PILGRIM

PILGRIM

*Risking the Life I Have to Find
the Faith I Seek*

Lee Kravitz

HUDSON
STREET
PRESS

HUDSON STREET PRESS
Published by the Penguin Group
Penguin Group (USA) LLC
375 Hudson Street
New York, New York 10014

USA | Canada | UK | Ireland | Australia | New Zealand | India | South Africa | China
penguin.com
A Penguin Random House Company

First published by Hudson Street Press, a member of Penguin Group (USA) LLC, 2014

REGISTERED TRADEMARK—MARCA REGISTRADA
HUDSON
STREET
PRESS

LIBRARY OF CONGRESS CATALOGING-IN-PUBLICATION DATA
Kravitz, Lee.
Pilgrim : risking the life i have to find the faith i seek / Lee Kravitz.
pages cm
Includes bibliographical references.
ISBN 978-1-59463-125-2
1. Kravitz, Lee. 2. Spiritual biography. I. Title.
BL73.K73A3 2014
204.092—dc23
[B]   2014001286

Printed in the United States of America
1 3 5 7 9 10 8 6 4 2

Set in Ehrhardt Mt Std
Designed by Leonard Telesca

Author's note: This is a work of nonfiction. Some names and identifying details have been
altered to protect the privacy of particular individuals. The events in the book are based on
the author's memories, recollections, and personal reportage. Any errors or distortions are
unintentional.

*Penguin is committed to publishing works of quality and integrity. In that spirit, we are proud to
offer this book to our readers; however, the story, the experiences, and the words are the author's
alone.*

To Elizabeth, Benjamin, Caroline, Noah, Pip, Mac,
Sophie, and Kit Nubbins:

May you be safe,
May you be happy,
May you be healthy,
May you live with ease.

Contents

part one

Rite of Passage

We don't receive wisdom; we must discover it for ourselves after a journey that no one can take for us or spare us.

—MARCEL PROUST

My Pilgrim Heart

When I met the woman who would become my wife, God didn't come up at all in our conversation. We talked about our jobs, the colleges we went to, why and when we first moved to Manhattan, Bill and Hillary Clinton, the Detroit Tigers (her favorite team), the Cleveland Indians (my favorite team), and our mutual dislike of the New York Yankees and Republicans. We talked about a lot of things . . . just not about God.

Our matchmaker, a publishing executive, had been one of my best friends in college and she knew Elizabeth, a literary agent, from the book business. In describing Elizabeth, she told me: "You'll love her. She's got pre-Raphaelite beauty, deep blue eyes, curly blond hair. She's got a career, not like those 'children' you've been dating all these years. And she's Jewish, which for you, after all your shiksas, will be a big change. I predict you'll be married in four months."

"What's the hurry?" I said with a laugh.

"You're thirty-nine . . . about to turn forty," she said. "Elizabeth is the one. Trust me. She's your best bet for happiness."

I met Elizabeth at a bar that had been a watering hole for generations of artists, writers, musicians, and sports stars, including Thomas Wolfe and the Bambino himself. Elizabeth was sitting by the window, sipping white wine. Her long blond curls brushed my face as she got up to hug me.

"You're allergic to cats," she said.

"How did you know?" I asked.

"I just do." She frowned. "You're not a cat person and I have two and they are not negotiable. We'll need to get over that."

If I could have foreseen the trajectory our relationship would take, I might have responded by asking, "Are you allergic to God?" But God was not even remotely on my mind that night.

Within minutes of meeting Elizabeth, I learned that she had grown up a mile from where my parents were living in Detroit; her mother shopped at the Loehmann's where mine worked as a sales-clerk and cashier; we both loved watching *Law & Order*, major-league baseball, and C-SPAN, especially the *Prime Minister's Questions* hour, which pitted Tony Blair against his Tory opposition in spitfire debate. Also, Elizabeth's Detroit-inflected *a*'s were even flatter than mine, which had been formed, or rather squashed, during my childhood in Cleveland.

We lived in speedy, glittery Manhattan, but, on that first date, it felt as though we were back in the Midwest of our childhood, sharing a milkshake in a malt shop. I had spent nearly twenty years wandering the world of exotic women and untenable relationships, but here, suddenly, I was with the girl next door. Like me, Elizabeth was Jewish and worked in a field related to publishing. We spoke the same language (literally, with those same flat *a*'s). We wanted the same number of children—three—and knew that to have them at our age, we would need to get busy soon. We seemed, at least on paper, to be ridiculously, miraculously right for each other.

Our second date took us to a Knicks-Pistons basketball game at Madison Square Garden. Elizabeth's boss had given her his tickets in the VIP section, which was right behind the Knicks' bench and filled with famously die-hard celebrity Knicks fans like Mike Bloomberg and Spike Lee. There was only one person in the section rooting for Detroit. Whenever a Piston blocked a shot or scored a point, Elizabeth would leap from her seat and cheer, drawing savage looks from Mike, Spike, and the players on the Knicks' bench. As uncomfortable as this made me feel, I also felt a surge of pride and excitement: Elizabeth was ballsy . . . and a head-turner.

I kept thinking: I have never felt so totally at ease with a woman. I imagined that if the two of us walked down the streets of our childhoods together, we'd have the profound sense that we'd walked those streets together before—and that everywhere we'd go in the future together, from a beach in Cancún to the corner grocery store, would be home.

At the subway that night, when we kissed and went our separate ways, the only question I had was whether it would take as long as four months for us to wed. Later, Elizabeth would tell me that she had been thinking the same thing.

God didn't enter the picture at all during our courtship. When he finally did, it would unsettle everything we felt so certain about in those early days, including that profound sense that we'd finally come home.

Each of us has a spiritual profile—a biography of belief and aspiration that is shaped, in part, by our birthright and upbringing. Mine begins in an impoverished Lithuanian shtetl during the last two decades of the nineteenth century. It was there that my paternal great-grandfather, Chatza Kravetz, grew up in a family of hard-working peasant farmers and devout Jews.

Like the characters in Sholem Aleichem's "Tevye" stories, Chatza's life and prospects were as precarious as the perch of a fiddler on the roof—prey to poverty, pogroms, and the threat of expulsion. When he was sixteen, Chatza was conscripted into the Russian army to fight alongside the same Jew-hating Cossacks who had been terrorizing his village. He fled to South Africa, where he worked in the diamond mines, fought in the Second Boer War, and dreamed of a better, less precarious life in America.

When he got here, in 1908, the official at Ellis Island who processed his papers changed his name to the Americanized "Charles Kravitz," although he still went by Chatza. He eventually moved his family to Cleveland, where he opened a grocery store. Spiritually, Chatza remained a Jew from the shtetl. He feared God. He lived by the Torah's commandments. He demanded that his children treat both him and my great-grandmother with unquestioning respect. He said his morning prayers. He kept the Sabbath holy. In shul he stood in the front row, swaying back and forth as he davened (prayed).

My Grandpa Benny—the first Kravitz born in America—dropped out of school after ninth grade to work in Chatza's grocery store. Ben dreamed of making it big. So he started a side business: selling corn sugar to bootleggers. When Prohibition ended in 1933, he used his sugar proceeds to begin a company that made rubber products for the auto industry; it made Ben and his three younger brothers and their families rich. Ben had little use for prayer and ritual, and worked all the time—even on the Sabbath. He gave generously of himself to Jewish charities and Israel but I never got the sense that he gave much thought to God.

Both my father and his brother Pudge grew up during the 1940s caring mostly about girls, baseball, and later, business. They bought homes in the suburbs and dreamed of sending their children to college so that we could become successful in the gentile world. My parents joined a synagogue and sent us to Hebrew school, but they did it mainly to please my grandparents.

On Friday nights we'd gather at my grandparents' home for Shabbat dinner. All sorts of family and friends would come for the freshly baked challah, homemade matzah ball soup, and roasted chicken. We'd say the blessings over the candles, wine, and bread. During dinner the older people would tease each other in Yiddish and kvetch about their aches and pains and young people. (Their gripe was that we didn't respect them enough.) After dinner we'd gather around the piano and sing along as my Aunt Fern played Yiddish folk songs and show tunes—some of my happiest memories. But by the time I was thirteen, the family business was failing, my grandfather and his brothers weren't speaking to each other, and the Shabbat dinners that had sustained our family's Jewishness were history. In the three generations preceding mine, it would have been unthinkable for a Kravitz to marry a man or woman who wasn't Jewish; in mine, only one would marry a Jew.

I was born eight years after the world learned the full extent of the Holocaust, and five years after the Jewish State of Israel was established on a vulnerable sliver of land in the Arab Middle East. During my childhood, the adults in my predominantly Jewish community talked endlessly of the piles of bones and eyeglasses the Nazis had left behind—and the lampshades the Nazis had made from the skin of Jews. In Hebrew school, we were taught that God was constantly testing our forefathers' obedience and love. We were his "Chosen

People," his "Light onto the World." That's why he demanded so much righteousness from us—and exposed us to so much persecution and pain. It was a heavy burden to bear. Whenever I attended services with my grandparents, the rabbi would end his sermons with a thundering command to give money to Israel so that we, the Jewish people, would "never again" be victims of a madman's whims. I could sympathize with that goal deeply, but the ferocity of his message, uttered over and over again, to the exclusion of anything even remotely relatable to my inner life as a thirteen-year-old, left me feeling spiritually empty and alone.

On Yom Kippur, the holiest day of the year, the light seemed to shine most brightly on the dresses and jewelry of the fashion queens who'd parade out the door and to the ladies' room as soon as the rabbi began his sermon. Throughout the service there was the constant buzz of women gossiping and men snoring. I, too, would doze off: The rabbi was preachy and overbearing, the God we prayed to seemed distant from my concerns.

On the day of my bar mitzvah, I did a reasonably good job of reading the Torah in the language of my ancestors in front of several hundred friends and relatives. But I felt no sense of accomplishment, only that I'd put on a good enough show.

I hated the hypocrisy of it all, the lack of anything that felt spiritual. By then I wanted more from religion. I wanted to feel inspired and lifted up.

High school was a challenging time for me: I injured my pitching arm, ending my dreams of playing pro or even college baseball and putting strains on my relationship with my father, who had pushed me to keep playing beyond the pain.

My father lost his job, and it would be years before he found a new one. My grandfather died of a massive heart attack. My mother was on the verge of a nervous breakdown; she relied on me to keep her from falling apart.

At night, the news was filled with sad and unsettling images: a nine-year-old girl running naked and screaming through the streets of Saigon; men pointing from a Memphis motel balcony in the direction of the shots that had just killed their prophetic leader; a politician of once-in-a-generation promise gunned down in the basement of an L.A. hotel; and everywhere, anger in the streets and ghettos burning.

It all hurt. And, like so many young people in America at the time, I was yearning for perspective, guidance, and someone to give me a reason why my life mattered.

It came in the form of an idealistic young priest who taught courses in philosophy and psychology at my high school. In Father Jarvis's classes we read Aristotle and Plato; Freud and Jung; Camus, Sartre, and Marx. We also read the New Testament and the new breed of Protestant and Jewish theologians who were challenging the antique image of God as heavenly father and king.

Until then, I had grown up in a spiritual and theological vacuum. Now I couldn't get enough of these great thinkers who had pondered the nature of God, man, and the universe. I'd read them early in the morning and late at night, on weekends and holidays, at the beach and in the park. And, even though I understood only a fraction of what they wrote, I was beginning to see the world differently through their spiritually attuned eyes.

Of everything I had read, the New Testament took the deepest hold of me. I imagined myself at the foot of a hill in Galilee, standing shoulder to shoulder with hundreds of Jews who felt as beaten down by the circumstances of their times as I did, listening to a fearless carpenter deliver a message so radical that it had the power to right wrongs, topple empires, and change the world:

"Blessed are the poor in spirit: for theirs is the kingdom of heaven. . . ."

"Blessed are they that hunger and thirst after righteousness: for they shall be filled. . . ."

"Blessed are the peacemakers: for they shall be called sons of God."

As difficult as it was for me to accept the notion that Jesus was the son of God by an immaculate birth, and that he died for our sins, and that he rose from his grave three days after his crucifixion, I found his ethic of selfless love far more deserving of my respect than the Old Testament Yahweh's cruel justice. Wasn't everyone in the world—including the poor and defenseless—as chosen as I was in God's eyes? Didn't every man and woman on earth have an equal right to strive for happiness and live in peace?

In the Ten Commandments, Yahweh gave gold stars for not killing, not stealing, and not coveting your neighbor's wife. Wasn't there even more merit in loving your neighbor, turning the other cheek, and going the extra mile, as Jesus had said?

I couldn't have cared less about his healing of lepers or walking on water or feeding the multitudes with a single loaf of bread. What drew me to him most was his fierce criticism of the holier-than-thou hypocrites who ruled the religious roost. He couldn't tolerate them any more than I could.

That spring, for our senior project, two of my classmates and I studied Eastern philosophy and religions. We were interested in expanding our religious horizons and experiencing what Eastern mystics meant when they talked about higher consciousness and at-oneness with God. To help us accomplish that, we decided to learn a technique called Transcendental Meditation, which had been in the news because celebrities like Mia Farrow and the Beatles had gone to India to study TM with its founder, the Maharishi Mahesh Yogi.

Later, in the 1980s and 1990s, the Transcendental Meditation movement would promise that TM could help you levitate and go to the place deep in your consciousness where the individual mind identifies with the Unified Field, the fundamental unity at the heart of all consciousness and the laws of nature. But in 1971, when I learned the technique at nearby Kent State University, its professed goals were more modest: As research at Harvard and UCLA had shown, TM could help you reduce stress, lower your metabolic rate, and reach a state of alert and relaxed openness that could make you more creative and improve every aspect of your life.

My initiation took place in an off-campus apartment. I was greeted at the door by a pretty young woman with long brown hair. She led me into a back room, where a man in his mid-twenties was standing in front of an altar to Guru Dev, the Maharishi's teacher. After lighting a stick of incense, he dropped to his knees and motioned for me to kneel down next to him and repeat a prayer of thanks to Guru Dev in Sanskrit. Then, rising to his feet, he gave me my personal mantra: "Eiyan." I repeated it over and over—out loud, then silently—until I was alone in the room and meditating with my eyes closed.

Thoughts would come, then go, with varying intensity. Whenever I became aware that I was thinking about something—the pretty assistant out front, a toilet flushing, the blue and green clouds that kept drifting by on the inside screen of my mind—I went back to silently repeating my mantra, as my initiator had instructed. The session lasted twenty minutes and at the end the assistant came in and said, "Now slowly open your eyes."

During the next six weeks I meditated twice a day. In general, I felt less anxious, restless, and judgmental, and more receptive, alert, and engaged. But whenever I tried to meditate at home, either in my bedroom or out in the yard, I faced a huge challenge: my disapproving mother, who saw no value in my sitting cross-legged with my eyes closed when there were umpteen chores for me to do: "Clean your room!" "Walk the dog!" "Finish your homework!" I'd pretend not to hear. Instead, I'd repeat my mantra louder and louder and faster and faster, defeating its central purpose of relaxing me.

According to the Maharishi, you are not supposed to share your mantra with anyone, not even your closest friend; if you do, you end up associating it emotionally with that person and tarnish its effectiveness. When my high school girlfriend threatened to break up with me if I didn't tell her "your magic word," as she called it, I gave in. I should have heeded the Maharishi's warning.

As the deadline for our senior project approached, I hadn't gotten even close to having a mystical experience, nor had my partners. So we decided to follow Aldous Huxley's example and open the "doors of perception" by taking a mind-altering drug—LSD.

We drove to pristine Amish country, far from the madding crowd. It took nearly an hour for the drug to take effect. I threw a pebble into a lake and it rippled into hundreds of self-replicating rhombuses. When I looked up, the farm across the road had morphed into a canvas of vibrating yellows, greens, and blues. The horizon began to dance beneath the sun. A dragonfly—or was it an angel?—landed on my shoulder and whispered into my ear.

About two hours into my trip I felt myself separating from my body and floating toward heaven. When I looked down, I could see my two friends huddling around my coffin. I was terrified.

As I started coming down from the acid, I felt great. I walked down the road toward a grove of shimmering apple trees. Everything—from the concrete on the road to the branches of the trees—was throbbing with what I took to be the gently pulsating energy of the universe. I wasn't afraid anymore. I felt peaceful. The tree in front of me started swirling around and around, like a roulette wheel. When it stopped spinning, there was a man standing upright in its branches wearing a golden robe and smiling at me. I smiled back. He stretched out his hands and beckoned me to join him. But before I could take a step forward, he was gone.

I had been hallucinating, of course. Still, I took this encounter with Jesus as a sign.

That fall, my first semester at college, was full of challenges and new experiences. Not least, there was the specter of a Selective Service draft that would determine whether my classmates and I would fight in Vietnam. Confused, I began looking to Jesus for guidance. At least once a week I'd visit a Catholic church near campus to light a prayer candle and ponder how Jesus would have responded to the moral challenges of the Vietnam War and racial unrest. On Sundays I attended services at the college's interdenominational chapel; they were led by a charismatic chaplain who was a leader in the peace movement.

It wasn't the chaplain's fiery sermons that moved me to seek his spiritual counsel; it was the Lord's Prayer. As a Jew, my practice had been to stay silent while the rest of the congregation recited it. But one Sunday I said it out loud: "Our Father, who art in heaven, hallowed be thy name. Thy kingdom come . . ." When I said the words "thy will be done," a jolt of lightning-like energy surged through my body and I started shaking.

The following day, I made an appointment to talk to the chaplain about converting from Judaism to Christianity. We ended up talking for ninety minutes. I told him how deeply connected I felt to my Jewish roots and history, but how alienated I'd become by the lack of anything spiritual or uplifting in my Jewish upbringing. I told him about Father Jarvis, the priest who had introduced me to the New Testament, and how Jesus had taken root in my imagination and conscience and become a role model for me. I also told him about the time I had seen Jesus in the apple grove, and how I had shaken uncontrollably the previous Sunday during the Lord's Prayer.

"Aren't those clear signs that I should convert?" I asked.

The chaplain leaned back in his chair and let out a big belly laugh. "I'm not laughing at you," he said. "I'm thinking about Jesus, how compelling he is, particularly in these times when our human existence is threatened by so many cowards and hypocrites."

"I know exactly what you mean," I said.

Then he leaned forward and looked sternly into my eyes. "Jesus may be the best model we have for courageous, righteous action," he said. "But before I can advise you to convert, I must first know what you truly believe. Do you believe that Jesus is the son of God, begotten of the Father, being of one substance with the Father?" he asked.

"I'm not sure," I said.

"Do you believe that he came down from heaven and was incarnate and made man for our salvation?"

"Not really," I said.

"Do you believe that he suffered, and on the third day he rose again, and ascended into heaven—that he'll come again to judge the quick and the dead? Do you believe in an afterlife, a kingdom without end?"

The fact was, I didn't believe any of that. It became clear that converting to Christianity wasn't the answer for me.

By my sophomore year in college, the spiritual hunger that had marked my teenage years was fading. I turned my attention to my studies and to what I'd do after college. I spent most of my twenties traveling overseas, trying on a variety of careers and relationships. When I finally settled on journalism, I treated it as my higher calling, working all the time. Whatever yearnings I had were on a way-back burner, simmering on a low, imperceptible flame.

And that's where God was in my life when I finally met the woman who would become my wife.

Everything happened so ridiculously fast. Less than two weeks after our date at the Knicks-Pistons game, Elizabeth moved Stan and Russell, her two cats, into my apartment for the "Big Test." Elizabeth had lived with cats all her life—she loved them, doted on them, thought so deeply and compassionately about them that she had written a successful book about them. Cats made her happy; they gave more meaning to her life. I, on the other hand, hated cats. I had been allergic to them since I was seven, and even a few minutes in their presence made me miserable.

There was a lot at stake in this feline trial period. If I could co-exist with Stan (a big black Burmese) and Russell (a short-haired tabby), Elizabeth would take the next big step and move in with me. If I couldn't, either I'd need to find a first-rate allergist or a new girlfriend.

My eyes itched, my throat narrowed, I sneezed, I wheezed, I coughed. My brain ached from Stan and Russell's constant meowing for food, fresh litter, and tummy rubs. But I never once complained to Elizabeth, and after those six challenging weeks (for me), she did what she had promised and moved in. I was confident that I could deal with my allergies later.

Meanwhile, within minutes of hearing that her daughter was going out with a "boy" whose parents lived in Detroit, Elizabeth's mother drove straight to her neighborhood Loehmann's to introduce herself to my mother, who was working at the checkout counter. "Hi, Phyllis. I'm Joyce Kaplan. Your son is dating my daughter," she said excitedly. At my mother's next break they went to a nearby restaurant for tea. It took only a few minutes for them to discover how much they liked each other and to promise that they'd stay friends for life "no matter what happens with the children."

We "children" were tickled by our mothers' budding friendship. But during the next several weeks we didn't let on that we were doing anything more serious than casually dating. Our mothers kept meeting for tea and enjoying each other's company, but they had no idea that Elizabeth and the cats had moved in with me or that we wanted to get married and begin making babies right away.

We got a marriage license one month earlier than our friend Liz had predicted we would. Our plan was to take August off from work and spend three weeks driving through southern France on our "honeymoon." When we got back, we'd go to City Hall and get married: no family, friends, or frills.

Provence was magical: quaint hotels, coffee-and-baguette breakfasts, afternoons spent looking at paintings by Van Gogh and Cézanne, then wandering through the landscapes that had inspired them. I photographed my bride-to-be—her hair pinned up, blond curls falling to frame her face—against pine forests, mulberry bushes, and fig trees. At night we filled our glasses with cassis and rosé and toasted our remarkable happiness and good luck.

On our way to the airport, we stopped at a tiny roadside jewelry shop and bought matching gold wedding bands, planning to marry at City Hall as soon as possible after our return. We figured it would take about a week for us to get organized enough to get there.

We never got there.

The phone rang as we were settling in to watch TV one night.

"Hello?" I said.

"Jonny's dead." It was Jamie, Elizabeth's brother. He told me that their oldest brother Jonny had just been killed in a car crash. As he shared more of the details—a drunk teen had crossed over the median, Jonny had died on impact—I didn't say a word to Elizabeth of what had happened. It would be best for Jamie to tell her the news himself, then for me to comfort her through the terrible days and weeks ahead.

Elizabeth was inconsolable. Jonny's death only deepened her pain at having lost the most important person in her life six years earlier: her father.

By all accounts, Teddy Kaplan had been a remarkably humble, principled, and brave man. A war hero, he had lost his arm while rescuing a soldier under his command at the Battle of the Bulge. He never complained or pitied himself. He felt blessed to be alive; to have Joyce as his wife and Jonny, Jamie, Michael, and Elizabeth as his children; to have colleagues he liked and good friends.

Teddy had a terrible voice but he loved singing along to recordings of Broadway shows with his similarly vocally challenged daughter. He taught her how to play golf and tennis, his favorite sports. He bought season tickets to University of Michigan football games, so that he and Elizabeth could cheer their team to victory.

Then, forty years after his amputation, the hepatitis C–tainted blood that had saved Teddy Kaplan's life took it away. He was only sixty-six when he died. And Jonny was only forty-four when he was killed. "It's not fair," Elizabeth kept crying. "It's not fair."

Some of the condolences that came in tried to assure Elizabeth that her brother was in a better place. "Bullshit," she said. People had said the same thing when her father died. "If anything proves that there's not a God, it's that Jonny is dead and that my father died before he could meet you and our children."

Elizabeth was born into a politically progressive, culturally sophisticated family that wouldn't even entertain the possibility of God. In fact, the Kaplans' rabbi—a brilliant iconoclast named Sherwin Wine—made national news in the early 1960s when he started the first ever "synagogue without God" in suburban Detroit. Sherwin loved his Jewish identity, food, and culture. But he had no use for Judaism's chauvinistic, autocratic God or its biblical miracles. Or the Torah, with its theocratic view of the world and society—and its "patriarchal regulations and sacrificial rules." That type of thinking was fine when Jews didn't know better, Sherwin said. But in the age of science and reason, it insulted Jews' intelligence. And it kept them from making the most of their talents and their lives.

Sherwin's prayer book featured meditations on courage, beauty, and love. His sermons celebrated Jewish music, literature, and art. On Jewish holidays, as rabbis throughout the world praised God and read from the Torah, Sherwin shunned God and the Torah, explaining instead the humanistic lessons embedded in Jewish history and culture.

While my own Jewish upbringing had left me feeling angry and uninspired and in search of something deeper and more authentic, Elizabeth reveled in the Humanistic Judaism of her childhood without feeling any need to question it. Like her parents and brothers, she was drawn to the parts of Judaism that celebrated human reason and dignity and gave them the values and rituals that bound them together as a family.

I subscribed to some of those same values: for example, Judaism's historical commitment to freedom and social justice. At the same time, I wasn't comfortable with an ideology that dismissed the possibility of a God on the basis of human reason. In my experience, reason only took a human being so far. That's why I stayed open to a God who was beyond my rational capacity to know.

Sherwin was brave, brilliant, and original in what he said. But, too often, his sermons took the form of history lectures and travelogues. They could be intellectually fascinating, but they never moved me to that place of mystery, deeper meaning, or awe I craved. At times, I wondered whether Elizabeth and her mother would have been less devastated by Jonny's death if they had been able to find comfort in something larger than themselves—in God, for instance—but I kept those thoughts to myself for fear of adding to their pain.

Two years after Jonny was buried, Elizabeth got pregnant—with twins. She and her mother agreed that it was time to end the grieving with a wedding.

On September 21, 1996, Elizabeth and I were married in the backyard of her childhood home under her father's favorite tree, with Sherwin officiating. The event couldn't have been sweeter or more meaningful. Elizabeth was six months pregnant and huge. As she waddled down the aisle, a trio of violinists from the Detroit Symphony played music by Vivaldi and Mendelssohn. Before he pronounced us man and wife, Sherwin placed his hand over Elizabeth's belly and blessed the two "special guests" who bore witness to our union in love.

Three months later Benjamin and Caroline were born. I already had fulfilling work, and now a wife and children I loved so deeply that I couldn't imagine living without them. Three years later, Noah was born. With the addition of new cats and dogs, our family life became even crazier and more fun. And exhausting, too, so that my longing for God—or at least my awareness of it—was at an all-time low. But within two years, it would begin to grow again.

It started, as it did with many Americans, in the days following the attack on the World Trade Center. That unthinkable act of terror, only miles from where we lived, shattered everything that Elizabeth and I had taken for granted about our safety and well-being. When I got home from my office the next evening, I found our four-year-old son stretched out on the living room couch—his eyes closed and fluttering, his legs tightly together, like Christ on the cross.

"What are you doing, Ben?" I asked.

"I'm dying," he said.

I reached down and cradled his head in my hands. "Why?" I asked.

"Because there are bad people killing good people," he said.

"Bad people are killing good people, Daddy. Are they going to kill us, too?"

Elizabeth and I had been trying our hardest to shield our children from the gruesome images in the aftermath of the attack, first by putting the television on mute, then by turning it off altogether. But somehow Ben had taken it all in—from the whispers in the room, the looks on our faces, the worry in our eyes.

And now—imagining the worst, trying death on for size—he wanted me to answer a question that had left me tongue-tied and sad for him and for the world: "Are those bad people going to kill us, Daddy?"

I told him what parents are supposed to say at such moments. I said, "There are bad people in the world. But most people are good. And Mommy and Daddy will protect you. Your teachers will protect you. The army and police will put the bad people in jail."

In truth, I doubted everything I had said. In this terrible new world where terrorists were hijacking planes and blowing up innocents—where we felt compelled to watch our backs and fear our neighbors—I felt inadequate to the task of keeping my children safe and happy.

I closed my eyes and cupped my face in my hands. *God,* I prayed silently, *I want my children to grow up good and kind and curious and trusting. I want them to be full of hope and not fear. O keep us safe.*

These last words came from a deep, unprompted place. When I was Ben's age, I would kneel by my bed at night and say the prayer my Aunt Fern had taught me: "Before in sleep I close my eyes, to Thee O God my thoughts arise. I thank Thee for Thy blessings all that come to us, Thy children small. O keep me safe throughout the night, so I shall see the morning light."

My instinct to pray after the World Trade Center attacks was no doubt an old reflex kicking into gear because I perceived a threat to my loved ones. It was also a shot in the dark, spurred by a feeling of nowhere left to turn. There was also something deeper and more consequential at play: I had never taken my own or any other religion seriously enough to build a reservoir of words, wisdom, and convictions that could guide me or my loved ones through a nightmare of this magnitude. I had no life philosophy or creed. No defined sense of ultimate meaning. No sure path to guide my way. When Jonny was killed, I was at a loss for words and gestures that might ease Elizabeth's pain. But my spiritual deficiencies weren't just evident in the face of tragedy. Walking down the street, I could be so self-involved that I wouldn't recognize an opportunity to be kind to a person in need. I'd let the smallest annoyances destroy my equilibrium and day. I was blessed with family, friends, money, and good health, but I felt empty and forlorn without a connection to something larger.

After that, I found myself praying from time to time for my children's safety. Later, I'd find myself speaking to someone I increasingly called "God." I'd talk to this God mainly in my head. But when no one was around, I'd talk to God out loud. I'd ask God for wisdom when I felt sad, and for guidance when I felt confused. And when I felt really happy—for example, when I watched my kids chase pigeons or butterflies in the park—I'd thank God for my blessings. I still couldn't say with total certainty that I believed in God, or could define what I meant by God, but I was aware of wanting this something or someone to be more present in my life.

I couldn't share any of my yearnings for God with Elizabeth or anyone else in my life. At work, virtually no one felt comfortable talking openly about their religious beliefs. And if religion was discussed at all in our Upper West Side social circles, it was to knock it—or to note how God-fearing fundamentalists were trying to take over the government and make life worse for everyone else.

The one conversation I did have with Elizabeth about my spiritual needs went like this:

"You've been looking depressed lately. What's wrong?" she asked.

"It's that feeling I get from time to time that I need more of a spiritual life."

"Aren't we enough?" she asked, referring to herself, the kids, and the life she had fashioned for us as a family.

"I love our life. It's amazing," I told her. "And so are you. It's just that sometimes I long for something deeper," I said, without actually referring to God. "That's not wrong, is it?"

She replied, "I just wish you could be happier with what we have right now."

As Ben and Caroline approached the age of nine, Elizabeth and I came to a critical juncture in our family's religious life.

Why nine?

Particularly in the Reform denomination of Judaism, nine is the age when parents typically make a decision about whether their children will be educated to have a bar (for a boy) or bat (for a girl) mitzvah, the coming-of-age ceremony at which Jewish thirteen-year-olds are invited to read a portion of the Torah in front of a congregation that includes their family and friends. Occasionally I'd hint at Ben and Caroline having a b'nai mitzvah—the name for a combined ceremony. But I never thought Elizabeth would go for it, particularly if it involved her children reading from what she considered a fictional book ascribed to a nonexistent God. Then, on my fifty-second birthday, she said, "I have a really special present for you."

"What is it?" I asked.

"A b'nai mitzvah for your children."

"I thought you were dead-set against their having one."

"I am," she said. "But I also love you and know how much you'll regret it if they don't have one."

She was right. I may have had very mixed feelings about my Jewish upbringing, but I wanted my children, who were born only two generations after the Holocaust, to know, acknowledge, and embrace their Jewish heritage—and to declare themselves publicly as Jews.

We faced a problem, though, in that neither of us belonged to a synagogue. We had gone as guests to all sorts of synagogues over the years—Conservative, Reform, Humanistic, and even Orthodox—but none of them felt right enough to join. Elizabeth disliked any service that praised or even referred to God, and I found most of the services we attended too prosaic and preachy, or inauthentic and watered down. It was clear that we would need to find a less traditional way to prepare the twins for their b'nai mitzvah.

After several months of searching, Elizabeth found a rabbinical student named Fred who was willing to teach the kids Hebrew and Jewish history without going overboard on the miracles and God. Once word leaked out, parents of several of Ben and Caroline's friends asked if their own nine-year-old kids could join the class. Like Elizabeth and me, many of these parents were ambivalent if not hostile toward organized religion; most were also dismissive of God. Still, they felt a strong enough tie to their Jewish roots that they wanted their kids to undergo the Jewish rite of passage.

Every Tuesday evening for four years, the Kaplan-Kravitz Hebrew School gathered around our dining room table. Fred had been the principal of a Jewish day school, so he knew how to keep the kids entertained and on task with games like Hebrew dodgeball and Old Testament Jeopardy, and by discussing current and personal events from a Jewish perspective. Meanwhile, we parents would sit around the living room gossiping and sipping wine.

At the end of the third year, Elizabeth and I faced another challenge: finding a venue for the b'nai mitzvah. The last thing we wanted was one of those expensive, DJ-orchestrated affairs. Our goal was to create an event that would be as true to our values as the way we had schooled the twins.

The b'nai mitzvah took place in an eighteenth century Quaker Meeting House near our home in upstate New York. To get to the Meeting House, Rabbi Fred, restricted from driving on the Sabbath, had to walk a mile past cow farms, a riding school, a Friends cemetery, and an Evangelical church. The twins read from a Torah scroll that Elizabeth had rented from an elderly Hasidic Jew on Manhattan's Lower East Side. The 150 guests, including 65 teens bused up from the city, followed along in a photocopied prayer book full of mostly secular readings, which they used to fan themselves in the suffocating heat.

After reading their Torah portions in Hebrew and then English, the twins spoke movingly about what their portions meant to them. Then Fred invited us to come up and tell Ben and Caroline what we thought of them on their momentous day. Elizabeth said what she'd been saying to them since the day they were born: "You're fabulous! I couldn't be more proud of you." And I told them how happy I was that they had been called to the Torah by a rabbi who knew them, before an assemblage of people who loved and appreciated them, in a ceremony that affirmed the heritage of their forefathers.

I predicted that Ben and Caroline would question their Jewish faith and heritage as they grew older, as I had. And that their desire to be authentic in their actions and beliefs might inspire them to explore other traditions.

"That's a good thing," I said. "Be skeptical of other peoples' truths, including those of your parents, teachers, and rabbi. Be open to other ideas," I urged. "The important thing will be to live according to what you've come to know and value through your own experience—and to be the best and most compassionate people you can possibly be."

All through the celebration, I kept thinking about my Aunt Fern, the member of my family who would have appreciated it most. Although she was twelve years older than me, Fern, who was my father's sister, had been my spiritual soul mate when I was younger: We'd share secrets and poems and ponder God and the meaning of life. As Fern grew older, she was the only Kravitz of her generation to genuinely care about living a Jewish life: She knew Yiddish, prayed all the time to God, and tried to keep the Sabbath holy by lighting the candles, saying the blessings, and abstaining from certain activities.

Fern would have loved being there, but I didn't invite her. Diagnosed in the 1950s as a paranoid schizophrenic, she had been confined to a special-care facility outside of Cleveland since 1994. Like everyone else in my family, I had long respected the doctor's orders that we have no contact with Fern lest we reawaken the type of painful memories that had led her, in the past, to try killing herself. But in 2008, when I was addressing some of my unfinished emotional business during the writing of my first book, I took the risk of visiting her. At first I didn't recognize her. She had lost her hair and teeth and weighed almost three hundred pounds. She couldn't walk or feed herself. She kept pointing out the nurses who were plotting to kill her. But she couldn't have been happier to see me; nor I her, beyond anything I had imagined. And so I kept visiting my aunt—at least twice a year and always on her birthday. If it had been possible, I would have flown her to New York for the twins' b'nai mitzvah and given her a front-row seat.

Thanks to Elizabeth and her birthday gift, I had done my job. I had given my children a grounding in their birthright religion, as well as my blessing to be skeptical and follow whatever path they might eventually choose. But as I watched them greet their friends outside the Meeting House, I was seized with a desire to begin practicing what I had just preached to them. My yearning for God had been increasing in intensity for years, but I had done nothing to embrace, declare, or honor it. Nor had I found a spiritual community or home. Now that the twins' rite of passage was over, I felt the need to embark on one of my own.

In the weeks after the b'nai mitzvah I found myself doing something that my wife and children considered odd, annoying, even crazy. Instead of looking for *Law & Order* reruns, as I usually did when I wanted to relax, I began channel-surfing for shows with a religious theme. On Sunday mornings I'd watch Joel and Victoria Osteen instead of *Meet the Press*. I'd tune in to whatever televangelist was on the Trinity Broadcast Network—Kenneth and Gloria Copeland, Benny Hinn, Creflo Dollar, T. D. Jakes. On one channel there would be a nun repeating the Hail Mary hundreds if not thousands of times while fingering her rosary. On another there would be a shapely young reverend with blond curls who was reputed to have been a porn star; now she was giving detailed biblical exegesis in

Latin and Greek. I'd watch reruns of Billy Graham and Oral Roberts calling people to God in huge stadiums, and Bishop Fulton Sheen praising his "four writers—Matthew, Mark, Luke, and John," while disparaging Darwin, Freud, and Marx.

As much as I hated their hucksterism, proselytizing, and hyped-up versions of God, I felt a kinship with the televangelists: Like them, I burned to have God at the center of my life. To ease this ache, I took to walking around our neighborhood and making a conscious effort to attune myself to God's presence in every person and situation I encountered. It's difficult to describe exactly what I saw or experienced on those "God walks," but I can offer a general picture: I was more aware of the way sunlight illuminated buildings and faces. I didn't see danger around every corner, or dodge situations that might disturb me, as I typically did. Time slowed way, way down, and I was more receptive to whatever came my way. Also, I felt simultaneously gracious and grateful; it was as if there were no boundaries between me and the people I passed. We were distinct but also one.

Mostly I was aware of how focused, calm, and buoyant I felt. It reminded me of an article I had just read in a newsmagazine. Neuroscientists at the University of Pennsylvania had scanned the brains of Buddhist monks to see if the thousands of hours they had spent praying and meditating had impacted their brain structure. It had. The prefrontal cortex—the part of the monks' brains responsible for concentration and decision making—was significantly more active than that of the average person. (This signifies more blood flow and stronger brain connections.) Neuroscientists at the University of Montreal had detected similar changes in the brains of praying nuns.

These and other studies were leading neuroscientists to speculate that the human brain is "hardwired" for spirituality and God—that there is a neural basis for both mystical experience and moral intuition.

Was it my "hardwiring for God" that led me to pray for my children's safety after the terrorists struck? Did the sight and sound of Benny Hinn and Creflo Dollar make my "spiritual neurons" fire up even as the rest of my brain told me to turn the channel?

Even more to the point: Was what I experienced, during my walks, my brain on God? What if I could get better at attuning myself to God's presence both within and around me? Would my moral behavior and intuition improve? Would I become more focused and calm, more forgiving and compassionate, more spiritually able and fulfilled?

I wanted to attune myself to God's presence in all things—this was quickly becoming my consuming desire—yet paradoxically the more I sought God, the more uncomfortable and alienated I felt around my family and friends. When I'd mention God around them, they'd change the topic to politics or sports. Or they'd steal a joke from Bill Maher: "Why do we always have to worship him? Let's face it, God has a big ego problem."

I'd laugh along. But I wanted to be around people who shared my yearning.

That fall I found myself feeling strangely vulnerable. A policeman gave me a parking ticket and I felt so deeply misunderstood that I couldn't stop reliving my conversation with him for days. When one of our cats died, I felt the loss as much as everyone else in the family did. Ben and Caroline started testing their new teenage boundaries with me; I got angry and sulked.

One night I felt a tightening in my chest; I couldn't breathe. Afraid that I was having a heart attack, Elizabeth called a doctor friend and asked if I should go to the emergency room. She asked Elizabeth a few questions and said that it sounded like I was having an anxiety attack, not a heart attack. Still, I couldn't get to sleep. As I lay awake in bed, I found myself grasping for comfort and guidance . . . and for that something I called God.

The next day I surfed the Internet to see if there were any diseases that matched my symptoms. Eventually I found myself browsing through sites I had previously bookmarked, and clicked on one called Beliefnet, which described itself as being for people who wanted to "find, and walk, a spiritual path that will bring comfort, hope, clarity, strength, and happiness" to their lives. After everything I had been experiencing, it seemed just what the doctor had ordered.

One of Beliefnet's key features—an interactive quiz called "Belief-O-Matic"—matched your beliefs about God, the afterlife, and other religious topics to the religions that shared those beliefs. The quiz was glib and full of disclaimers, but I found its twenty questions—and the spiritual snapshot it produced of me—exhilarating.

Q1: What is the number and nature of the deity (God, gods, higher power)? I reviewed my choices. I didn't believe in multiple gods or goddesses, or in a single paternalistic God who looked down on us from heaven, or in no God at all (which would have been Elizabeth's choice). The answer that best matched my current understanding of God was, *(d) The impersonal Ultimate Reality (or life force, ultimate truth, cosmic order, absolute bliss, universal soul), which resides within and / or beyond all.*

In answering the second question, about life after death, it was clear that I didn't believe in a literal heaven and hell or a physical afterlife, yet I was willing to entertain the possibility of a spiritual existence beyond life, perhaps as a spark of consciousness that survives and endures.

A question on the origins of evil revealed that I didn't believe that wrongdoing resulted from Adam and Eve's original sin, or from not knowing our true spiritual nature. I attributed it to egotism—the feelings of self-importance and entitlement that lead to the desires, cravings, and attachments that cause people to steal, cheat, and kill.

There were also questions probing my beliefs about suffering, prayer, abortion, gender equality, the environment, healing, and war.

It was the question about war that gave me the most pause, just as it had nearly forty years earlier when I faced the prospect of being drafted. *Q18: Nonviolence (e.g., pacifism, conscientious objector) should be fundamental.* Did I think that statement was true or false?

Forty years earlier, I had determined that I was a conscientious objector to all war based on my fundamental religious beliefs. Since then, I had gone back and forth on the matter. I certainly believed that nonviolence and respect for human life was essential; otherwise, how could we live in peace or up to our fullest human potential? But I also knew that I would probably use every means available, including violence, to defend my family if I had to.

The quiz took me about an hour to complete, then Belief-O-Matic computed my answers and offered me a list of twenty-seven religions in order of their compatibility with what I believed. The results were fascinating. My beliefs matched up best with Unitarian Universalism, liberal Quakerism, mainline to liberal Christian Protestantism, and Mahayana Buddhism. Unlike Catholicism, Eastern Orthodoxy, and the Conservative Judaism of my youth, the religions that best complemented my beliefs placed little importance on dogma and ritual; they weren't "priestly" or hierarchical; they put meditation and mindfulness at the center of worship and daily life.

It seemed like a silly way to get me thinking about my true spiritual identity, but the Belief-O-Matic quiz helped me frame the conversation that had already been going on inside my head. Also, the list of my "most compatible" religions reminded me of the wealth of spiritual traditions that were available to me within minutes of our apartment. In our neighborhood I could find Pentecostal, Methodist, and Roman Catholic churches; a Zen Buddhist temple; an Orthodox Jewish shul; and congregations of Seventh-Day Adventists, Jehovah's Witnesses, and Latter-Day Saints. I could also find the towering cathedrals of Riverside Church and Saint John the Divine, the Jewish Theological Seminary (which trained Conservative Jewish rabbis), and the Union Theological Seminary (which trained theologians and clergy from various Christian denominations and Buddhists, too). There also were places where people meditated, did yoga, and worked for social justice as part of their commitment to God, including a building nicknamed the "God Box" because it housed so many of these pro-social religious groups.

The idea of sampling a variety of these spiritual practices and traditions excited me. In the religion of my birth, which I checked off as my own whenever I filled out a form, I felt like a spiritual misfit, at odds with Judaism's fundamental concept of God. I wasn't sure where I would end up finding my spiritual home, but for now I needed to distance myself from Judaism and its language for God and try on new ways to pray and get closer to the Divine.

I wasn't alone in my desire to explore other traditions and find a community that shared my evolving views of religion and God. According to the 2007 Pew survey of the American religious landscape, more than a quarter of the nation's adults had left the faith in which they were raised for either another religion or no religion at all. That figure jumped to an astounding 44 percent of all American adults if you factored in those who had changed from one type of Protestant-ism to another.

Even more telling, the number of American adults who identi-fied themselves as being unaffiliated had more than doubled in the last thirty years—to 16 percent. They included atheists, agnostics, the secular unaffiliated, and the religious unaffiliated. They were by far the fastest-growing group on the country's religious landscape.

Spiritually, we had become a country in flux—a nation of search-ers. And yet, there were very few role models for those of us looking for a more authentic spirituality in contemporary American life.

In the Hindu religion, men are expected to devote themselves to God and the spiritual aspect of their lives as soon as they've com-pleted their obligations as head of their household, usually around the age of forty-nine. It's not a cop-out for spiritually inclined Hindu men to leave their families and spend their remaining years "dwelling in the forest" and communing with God; it's considered their natural, spiritually inspired calling.

My midlife longing for God told me that there was a natural, perhaps biological progression to my spiritual needs—but my life as I had lived it had put me out of sync with them. Like many men and women in my generation of Americans, I didn't get married and have children until relatively late. As a result I would be putting my children through college until 2022, when I'd be nearly seventy years old.

I couldn't wait that long. I would need to search for a spiritual home and God within the context of my life as a father, husband, and payer of bills. I couldn't even think of traveling to an ashram in

India or a monastery in Greece. Any dancing with dervishes I'd do would need to take place within a hundred miles or so of New York City; otherwise, I wouldn't be able to be a full participant in the rich family life that meant so much to Elizabeth and me.

Could I pull that off? Could I, in effect, shop for God—and pursue a more contemplative life—in an apartment filled with the distractions created by three teenagers, two dogs, two cats, and the menagerie of friends and neighbors who were always coming over to visit? And what if my spiritual quest was successful? Would I find myself being pulled in directions that would take me away from the people I loved?

The immensity of these challenges was immediately clear to me. Since childhood, I had made a point of getting in shape for big games, important meetings, arduous journeys. Now I needed to get in shape for my spiritual quest. So I decided to start meditating again, using the mantra-based TM technique I had learned at Kent State. Because my original mantra had been saddled with so many negative associations—my mother's skepticism, my girlfriend's insistence on knowing it, my thirty years or so of not meditating—I started using a mantra I found in a book: "Sohum," which is Sanskrit for "I am that which is all there is." Saying it reinforced my feeling that God was within me and everyone else.

My goal was to meditate for twenty minutes twice a day: at 6:00 A.M., when the kids were still asleep, and at 4:00 P.M., before they got back from school.

The first time I tried meditating in the morning, our dogs Mac and Pip sensed that I was awake and began scratching at the bedroom door, asking me to take them out to pee. Then Sophie, meowing, jumped onto the bed and into my lap for her morning cuddle. Then Caroline turned on the light because she needed to see her outfit in our bedroom mirror and get feedback on how she looked: a taste of the challenges ahead.

My plan had been to follow Belief-O-Matic's recommendations, starting with Unitarian Universalism. Then I'd sample the next three religions on my list: liberal Quakerism, mainline to liberal Protestantism, and Mahayana Buddhism.

But on the first Sunday in November, one of my upstairs neighbors knocked on our door and said something that led me to change that plan.

"Elizabeth tells me that you're interested in learning more about Quakerism," she said. "Would you like to come to a meeting this morning with me?"

My spiritual shopping expedition was about to begin.

part two

Season of Silence and Awakenings

Let us be silent, that we may hear the whispers of the gods.

—RALPH WALDO EMERSON

Seeking the Light Within

January Through April

I thought I knew everything about Katherine, or at least as much as anyone could know about a neighbor and close family friend for nearly ten years.

She and her husband Robert live two floors above us with their daughter, Abigail, who is the same age as Ben and Caroline. Our two families have been gathering weekly in our living room or theirs since the children were seven to watch the latest episode of *American Idol*, and, when our allegiances shifted, *Glee*.

Katherine is what Elizabeth calls "a grown-up," an empathetic friend you can depend on to help you solve problems and get through the day. She has bright green eyes, auburn hair, and a huge smile that pushes you to keep on going when you're about to give up or fall apart.

Katherine's family literally came over on the *Mayflower*. She is descended on her mother's side from Elder William Brewster, the spiritual leader of the Pilgrims. Brewster named his daughters Patience, Fear, Love, and Wrestling. But when it came to naming her own daughter, Katherine found inspiration in another ancestor, Abigail Hinman, a raven-haired beauty who fired her musket at the traitor Benedict Arnold during the Revolutionary War.

Like most of our friends, it took a while for Katherine to find her place in the world. She had dreamed of becoming an actress, but after years of waiting on tables, she enrolled in culinary school and began working for a local green market, then in many of New York City's top kitchens, culminating in a stint as chef at a four-star restaurant. A year before we became her neighbors, Katherine was hired to manage the test kitchen at TV's Food Network. It was a fabulous job, especially for those of us who were lucky enough to be her friends. Each Christmas she'd bake a Smithfield ham that was so tasty you'd take one bite and hear angels sing; for the twins' b'nai mitzvah, she made a stuffed arctic char that was so delectable even the teenagers devoured it.

So I thought I knew a lot about Katherine—and I did. But there was one thing I didn't know about her until she knocked on my door that Sunday: For over ten years, Katherine had been on a spiritual journey that paralleled my own. I shouldn't have been so surprised. Most of us live compartmentalized lives and don't give even the people closest to us more than a slight glimpse of our spiritual yearnings. We assume they won't be interested—or that they'll think less of us if we do.

When I opened the door, it was 10:38 A.M. I was still in my pajamas.

"If you want to come, you'll have to get ready right away," Katherine said.

"Do I need a sport coat?"

"This isn't a wedding," she laughed. "Or a bar mitzvah. And,

OMG, even if it were: These are Quakers, Lee. Just wear jeans, a sweater, and your warmest coat. We only have fifteen minutes to get there."

I dressed exactly as Katherine had directed—and quickly. It was so windy outside that it took the two of us and also Gus the doorman to push open the building's revolving door. I put my hand on Katherine's back, then hurried her across the street. Even on a warm spring day it could take us at least ten minutes to walk the ten long blocks to 120th Street, and I didn't want to be responsible for our being late. As we pushed ahead in the wind, I tried to remember the little I knew about Quakers: their stance against war; the man with the wide-brimmed hat on the Quaker Oats box; Gary Cooper awkwardly referring to his neighbors as "thee" and "thou" in the movie *Friendly Persuasion*; the painting *Peaceable Kingdom* by Edward Hicks.

Hadn't Richard Nixon of all people been a Quaker? And William Penn?

I had always gotten the Quakers confused with the Shakers and Amish. I wasn't even sure whether Quakers considered themselves Christian or not. But I did know that when I took the Belief-O-Matic diagnostic quiz, liberal Quakerism (whatever that was) had come out near the top of the religions compatible with my beliefs, right behind Unitarian Universalism and ahead of Protestantism and Mahayana Buddhism.

I told this to Katherine.

"How cool!" she said.

"And how cool that you knocked on my door this morning. You'd told us that you were thinking of sending Abigail to a Quaker school," I said, "but I had no idea that you were a Quaker."

"I'm not," she said. "When my sisters and I were growing up,

Mother tortured us into attending Sunday school at her Congregational church. She also sent us to a Quaker high school. Not because we were Quakers, but because she was impressed with their values. That's when I first experienced a meeting—in high school—and I loved it. In a few minutes you'll see why."

The Morningside Meeting, as it was called, was held in Riverside Church, a neo-Gothic cathedral that towers nearly four hundred feet over Harlem and the Morningside Heights section of Manhattan's Upper West Side. Riverside's interdenominational American Baptists and United Church of Christ congregation had long been among the most progressive in the country. Fiery ministers like Harry Emerson Fosdick and William Sloane Coffin Jr. had preached against racism, injustice, and nuclear war from its pulpit. And it was here at Riverside, in 1968, that the Reverend Martin Luther King Jr. had first declared his opposition to the Vietnam War.

As we walked through the lobby, we could hear shouts of "Amen" and "Hallelujah" from Riverside's huge gospel choir. The sweet smell of incense wafted through the corridor as the new arrivals, dressed in their Sunday best, greeted each other with hugs and backslaps. "Amen." "Hallelujah." "Praise the Lord." The contrast with what I was about to experience couldn't have been greater.

We took the elevator up twelve floors. The door opened into a narrow hallway with a rickety sign-in table. Following Katherine's lead, I wrote my name in purple Magic Marker on a piece of recycled scrap paper, then slipped it into a plastic name-card holder, which I pinned to my shirt. We hung our coats in the makeshift cloakroom. Then we walked through the door, into the hushed meeting room, and sat in the back row.

The chairs were arranged in three concentric circles, so that each person could see the faces of several if not most of the other people in the room. There didn't seem to be anyone in particular leading the meeting. Most of the thirty or so people in the room had their eyes closed. There were several academic-looking types, with gray beards and round eyeglasses; a few working-class types, with muscular bodies and large hands; and a handful of students.

I closed my eyes. When I did, I became even more aware of the wind, which was hissing past the tower, amplifying the quiet—and cold—in the room. For the next hour, no one said a word. Then a woman in a thick plaid shirt stood up and asked if anyone had any thoughts they'd like to share. "Please feel encouraged to say whatever you'd like," she said. "But remember: When one of us finishes speaking, the rest of us should refrain from saying anything in response. Our tradition is to sit in respectful silence until the next person feels compelled to speak."

The gray-haired woman sitting across from me got up slowly to speak. "Today is the seventh anniversary of my dog's death," she said softly. "I still miss him."

It was clear, from the faces in the room, that most of us felt her pain.

"If I had said this to my children this morning, they would have mocked me," she said. "They would have told me to forget Beau and move on. But here," she said, "I can express how sad I feel without anyone judging me. This is a tremendous comfort."

After a few seconds a middle-aged Hispanic man got up. He said that he had just gotten out of prison. "I have been thinking all morning about my two young grandchildren," he said. "I will be meeting them and holding them for the first time today. I am so excited to see them," he said. "But I am also scared."

The woman who stood up next to speak had dark skin and broad features. She said that she was "a proud descendant of the Mayan people"—and that she had just moved to New York City from Florida. In her whole life, she said, she had never experienced such cold. "It got me thinking how you need the hot weather to appreciate the cold and the cold to appreciate the hot. Life is like that," she said. "Hot and cold, pleasure and pain, good and bad, you need the one to appreciate and understand the other."

The final speaker was a man about my age who said he taught first grade at a Quaker elementary school. "Earlier this week, when we were discussing the nature of God in class, this beautiful little girl said, 'God is the wind.' That's what I've been thinking this morning: how God is the wind, challenging us, enveloping us, breathing life into our days."

In this Quaker meeting—my first—I had some powerful thoughts of my own, even though I didn't share them. I was thinking about how different this had been from the worship services of my youth, where the rabbi would stand before our well-heeled congregation and warn that our ancestral religion would "die off" unless we gave money to Israel and made sure that our children married Jews.

I was thinking about how long I had yearned for a place like this where I didn't feel judged or preached at, where I could pray from the heart and experience an hour of inner peace. And I was thinking: Will it be here—in this wind-battered room, among these gentle, earnest people—that I finally find God and my spiritual home?

After the meeting I didn't have a chance to discuss these thoughts with Katherine—she was out the door and off to an event at Abigail's school. But before I headed home, I grabbed every piece of free literature I could about Quakers—or the Friends, as they preferred to be called—including a copy of the book *Faith and Practice*, which described their core beliefs.

When I got home, Elizabeth was full of questions: "How did you like it? Did you talk to anyone? Did you see anyone you knew besides Katherine? What did you like best about it? Anything you didn't like?"

My responses—"Great. No. No. Lots. Nothing"—were less than generous. I was aware of that. Her questions seemed casual and trivial next to the large and compelling truths I'd been exposed to that morning. But that wasn't the only reason I shirked her questions and turned on the football game instead. Like the woman at the meeting who missed her dog, I was afraid my loved ones wouldn't share my spiritual concerns if I bared my heart to them.

I had been struck by the simplicity and transparency of my first Quaker meeting. In stark contrast to the synagogue spectacles of my youth, it wasn't scripted or mediated by a minister or rabbi; also, no one stood center stage, telling you what to feel or do.

You didn't need to know an ancient language, or wear a special head covering or prayer shawl, to feel holy. There were no icons or stained-glass windows to distract you with myths and miracles. Or towering naves to pull your eyes and prayers up to heaven.

I liked all that. In the spartan setting of the Quaker meeting, in that hour of unremitting silence, you attuned yourself to the joys and sorrows, the fears and yearnings, percolating in the quiet depths of your heart. Your thoughts might not be formed yet; they might be struggling, in their sincerity, to be born. But you knew that you could stand up and speak without fear of being ignored or put down.

Who were these plainly dressed people who worshipped in respectful silence and shared the full spectrum of their emotions so tenderly with each other? What was the theology behind how they acted and what they said?

I began my study of Quakerism with the autobiography of George Fox, the seventeenth century reformer who founded the Religious Society of Friends. He had been dismissed by some historians as a "mystical hippie of his day." Fox was certainly mystical: He believed that he could obtain unity with God by apprehending spiritual truths that were beyond his intellect. But he wasn't a navel-gazer. Fox spoke out against religious corruption and hypocrisy; his goal was to make the Christianity of his time more personally relevant, authentic, and alive.

Born in 1624, he grew up in Leicestershire, a town in the English Midlands. "In my very young years," he wrote, "I had a gravity and stayedness of mind and spirit not usual in children." He described himself as being "alert to the wickedness" he saw in society and other people. He apprenticed as a shoemaker, but only for a short time. In the summer of 1643, "at the command of God," he left home, breaking off "all familiarity or fellowship with young or old," to wander throughout England preaching God's word. As his confidence grew, he began speaking out against the Church of England: "The Lord showed me, so that I did see clearly, that he did not dwell in these temples which men had commanded and set up, but in people's hearts . . . his people were his temple, and he dwelt in them."

Fox's great realization was that "there is that of God in every person." He had other names for it: the "Seed," the "Inward Light," the "Inner Light," the "Holy Spirit," the "Christ Within." But "that of God in everyone" encapsulates the spirit of his realization best, because once you internalize that idea you begin to see everyone in the world differently, as kin and brethren, as fellow sufferers, worthy of the love and respect you want for yourself.

Fox insisted that a Quaker's outward behavior be an expression of his inner convictions and beliefs. He urged "plainness" in dress, word, and deed. Believing all men equal under God, he and his fellow Quakers addressed every single person, including the wealthy, by "thee" and "thou"—the familiar forms of "you" in seventeenth century England. It was standard in polite society for people to bow to priests and take off their hats in the presence of people with authority. Quakers didn't do such things. Nor did they flatter people or give eulogies when people died. If they had, they would have been guilty of giving undue praise and stature to some people over others. Quakers didn't take oaths, not even loyalty oaths to king and country. For these and other "affronts," they endured "blows, punchings, beatings and imprisonments." Fox himself went to prison eight times.

I was struck by their courage and integrity: Against fierce opposition, the Quakers stood by their values and ideals that were centuries ahead of their time. Their belief in "the Christ Within" led them to testify against slavery, war, and the barbarity of the penal system. If all persons were equal in God, how could one man own another man? Or be put in the position to kill another man on the battlefield? Or be deprived of a second chance to achieve his divinely human potential, even if he'd committed a crime? And the Quakers insisted that all of these rights, privileges, and principles applied to women, too.

"To walk gladly over the earth answering that of God in every person." This was Fox's prescription for leading a meaningful life. I had started taking that wonderful medicine during my "God walks" through my neighborhood. As I looked for God in everyone I encountered, I became calmer, more open, and less afraid. The next step spiritually would be to begin "answering that of God" in every person. Before I could do that, however, I would need to become much more skilled at listening and responding to other people, attuning myself to their emotional truths and needs.

It was the Quaker concept of God that excited me most about the religion as revealed in Fox's writings. But when I told that to Katherine, she said, "That's what troubles me most about Fox: all that God stuff."

Katherine didn't consider herself an atheist, but she didn't like when people used the word and idea of God ubiquitously and reverentially to bring them riches and eternal life or to court votes or to proclaim their superiority over other people. "I consider myself a humanist, like your wife," she told me. But Elizabeth would never be comfortable in a place where people prayed or referred lovingly to God. So I asked Katherine, "How did you end up at the Morningside Meeting, in the company of so many people who are listening so intently for God?"

"It started with the Vietnam War," she said. "One day, close to my Quaker high school, the police rounded up thousands of nonviolent protesters and took them to jail. It was inspiring to be at an educational institution that said, 'This is wrong'—that encouraged its students to hate war and work for peace. Twenty years later, in 1990, when the first President Bush launched Operation Desert Storm, I found myself getting angry again. And sad."

Katherine saw the war as a cynical attempt to protect and control the flow of Middle East oil, with terrible consequences for the hundreds of thousands of Iraqis and Kuwaitis who were killed and left homeless. But the vast majority of Americans supported the Gulf War, and as Bush's approval ratings climbed to 90 percent, Katherine felt marginalized. And alone. Until she heard about and attended the Morningside Meeting. "Week after week, we held the struggle against the war in the Light. I was sitting among people who felt as strongly as I did that the war was wrong—that war is never a solution." The fact that many of those people looked to God for guidance meant less to Katherine than their activism, sense of service, and their heartfelt opposition to the war.

After the war ended, in April of that year, Katherine felt less need for the Morningside Meeting. She began attending sporadically, then not at all. By the time she got pregnant with Abigail, in 1996, she hadn't been to a meeting in years; nor did she return while Abigail was a young child.

"So what brought you back?" I asked.

"Getting older," she said. "As I got closer to fifty, I realized that I had accomplished my career and family goals but what else was there? I was feeling a sudden spiritual vacuum. Nothing I tried—travel, fasting, I even visited a friend at an ashram—seemed to fill it. There was all this chatter in my head. I needed to quiet it down."

In July 2010, she heard about a Quaker meeting that took place in Battery Park, at the southern tip of Manhattan. Every Thursday evening, a small group of people gathered in a secluded area of the park called the Labyrinth for Contemplation. The labyrinth, a walking path that formed seven circular rings, had been created to commemorate the one-year anniversary of the World Trade Center tragedy, and it was meant to be a place for meditation and healing.

"The day I went, there were two people sitting on a bench, next to a flag with a peace sign on it. I sat down next to them. And for the next hour we just sat there, in silence, looking at the boats in the harbor and the Statue of Liberty, which was bathed in this amazing sunlight. It was so incredibly peaceful. We were three strangers but we had created this wonderful, sacred space for ourselves. And I had this profound sense of coming home to a place where I wanted and was meant to be."

That was the experience that prompted Katherine to start going to the Morningside Meeting in Riverside Church again: "The room in which we gather is stripped down, bare, devoid of any affectation," she told me. "But the experience I get here every Sunday is luxurious, better than any spa."

I asked her to elaborate.

"For most of my life I've been the person in charge, the one who is driving the bus and telling everyone what to do. Here I don't have to say or do anything. And I can be a student to an amazing community of people who are a lot wiser than me."

She paused, then smiled to herself.

"What's so funny?" I asked.

"How the elevator makes a 'ding' noise whenever someone gets off on the twelfth floor. It reminds me of that famous line in the movie *It's a Wonderful Life*: 'Every time a bell rings an angel gets its wings.' There's this funky group of characters here—ex-prisoners, people on welfare, professors, millionaires. And each of these people is different and unique and not who you think they are. It's a subtle and caring community. A community of . . . angels."

A community of angels who gather every Sunday in a connected silence that has a very different impact on them than they get praying or meditating alone. Often a theme will emerge over the course of the meeting as people rise to speak.

"When I started going to Morningside again, my biggest 'aha' moment was realizing how each week's themes were such a strong reflection of what I had been thinking about or struggling with all week. There was almost a freakishness in the harmonics of where I was and where the meeting was and how the meeting would speak to me."

I would see what Katherine meant on a foggy Sunday morning in February. All along Riverside Drive, the subtle gradations of gray were broken only by the ghostly march of skeletal trees and hulking apartment buildings. It was obvious to me that she was in a low mood, and I asked why.

"It's been a tough few weeks," she said.

Katherine and Robert hadn't found an effective way of helping Abigail with her ever-increasing workload at school. At the same time, Katherine's mother's dementia was getting worse. Katherine would need to find a better way of organizing her mother's medications—and making sure that she took them. "And how in the world am I going to persuade her to stop driving and surrender her license?" she said. "I really have no clue."

Next to Katherine's troubles, mine seemed small. And yet I had them. For example, all winter I had been looking forward to the start of Ben's baseball season. But now he was telling me that he was tired of playing baseball and wanted to run track instead. "The kids who play baseball are boring," he said. "The cool kids run track." I hated it when he talked like that. The more he quoted his "bros"—older boys he had begun to emulate—the less I recognized him. Sure, Ben was doing what I and every adolescent boy in history had done—figure out who he was and how he would present himself to the world. Still, I didn't like it. I was losing my ability to influence my son, and it depressed me. I carried the sadness I had been feeling all week because of Ben's decision into that morning's meeting.

When the meeting officially started, at 11:00 A.M., I closed my eyes. Attuning myself to the silence within me, I became aware of distant car horns, the scrape of a foot on the floor, Katherine's quickening breath. In my readings over the past several weeks, I had come across several principles that both intrigued me and enlarged my understanding of what I would be experiencing during the meeting.

The Inward Light (or Seed, Inner Light, and so on) helps us to discern between good and evil; it presents us with alternatives and guides us in making choices.

When someone says they are "minding the Light," it means that they are noticing, listening for, or paying heed to it.

When someone asks the Meeting to hold a person or problem "in the Light," they are asking for God's presence to illuminate, or shed light on, that person or problem.

At the heart of Quakers' worship is what they refer to as the "healing power of solitude." Through the Quaker meditative technique of "centering down," worshippers learn to still or direct their conscious thoughts so that they can see themselves and their problems more clearly. Theists might use this technique to sense the inward presence of the Holy Spirit or to ready themselves to hear the still small voice of God whispering into their soul's ear, as they refer to it; theists and nontheists alike might use it to quiet the negative and confusing chatter inside their heads. Centering down can be accomplished in any of a number of ways: for example, by meditating on a single word like "love" or "God"; thinking about a biblical story or passage; recalling a meaningful event or encounter; holding a person or problem in the Light; or visualizing an inspiring painting or piece of music.

Sometimes no one will speak during a meeting for worship, but usually at least one or two people stand up and share a story or their thoughts. Those who do aren't just speaking *to* the other people in the room; they are speaking *for* them—for their spiritual "seekings" and needs, according to Quakers.

Spoken ministry is a serious matter. It demands waiting before you talk and making sure you have something to say; it means speaking clearly, concisely, and loud enough for everyone, especially the older people in the room, to hear.

One of my favorite Quaker writers, Richard Francis Allen, advised people who attend meetings to avoid "emotional outbursts, prepared speeches or off the top of the head rants," especially when they involve divisive topics like politics. He had guidelines for listeners, too: Be prepared to hear much that will mean little if anything to you. Be patient, especially with speakers who are struggling to articulate themselves. "Accept one another's revelations with tender hearts, knowing that anyone can speak truth" and that "a simple thought, briefly expressed by a timid speaker, may be the message most needed" by someone else.

From my studies I had gained a Quaker 101–level knowledge of what I might experience during the next ninety minutes of silent and spoken ministry. Because I was familiar with the rhythm and structure of the meeting for worship, I could better appreciate its nuances and deeper meanings. Because I knew the key concepts, I found myself listening to what other people said with more compassion, awake to the truths that might be embedded in what they said.

However, it was still hard for me to sit quietly and meditate, just as it was for me at home. I felt antsy, distracted, and sleepy at times. My mind would race from one thought to another. Instead of focusing inward, I'd find myself opening my eyes and scanning the room for details I could use in my journal—I had honed those skills as a journalist. The problem was, I had been trained as a reporter to be skeptical and objective, not open and receptive to God's promptings. It struck me that taking notes, even mental ones, might hurt my chances of finding God.

After fifteen minutes or so, my thoughts convened around Ben's decision to run track. Why did I have to take it so personally? Was I just "being Harry" again—our family code phrase for behaving like my father? Harry had pushed his four sons through injury and pain to play football, with terrible consequences for our bodies, our psyches, and our relationships with him. Was I doing something similar to Ben by looking so miserable when he told me that he wouldn't be trying out for baseball? Maybe it was just my time as a parent to get my heart broken. So many of my friends had told me of the pain they experienced when their children moved away, didn't call from college, dated a boy or girl they didn't like, stopped wanting to visit them. It comes as inevitably as death: Your children break your heart and you need to learn to live with the pain.

When I said that to myself, it felt as though I had come upon a universal truth that might be useful to other worshippers at the meeting: Should I stand up and share it? I said it to myself again— *Warning to all parents: If your child hasn't broken your heart yet, he or she inevitably will.* Now I wasn't sure. If I said this "truth" out loud, would it have any real meaning for the others in the room? Or would they think that I was being self-pitying and a show-off?

I came up with several other reasons for not sharing the thoughts that had just seemed so powerful to me: My story would go on too long, it would need too much context, it was the type of thing my father might say, it ultimately would be of no interest or benefit to anyone in the room.

The moment passed.

By then, the youngest person in the room was standing up and getting ready to speak. She was maybe twenty years old and was wearing her light brown hair pulled back over a Columbia University sweatshirt. "My mother and I had an adventure this week," she said. "For some reason, we kept our Christmas tree up much longer than usual. I'm not sure why, other than why waste it once you've put it up. Also, it kept sprouting green stuff so it seemed wrong to just get rid of it. But we finally did."

She paused and breathed in so deeply that her glasses inched down over her nose. Then she resumed her story: "We took the tree outside on Tuesday and chopped it up. When we did I was aware of how green it was inside, how alive and resilient, even after it was dead. It made me aware of the life and resilience in all of us."

Somehow, the woman's story had set a theme in motion. In the part of the meeting where members share their joys, sorrows, and any lingering concerns, a man who looked to be in his mid-sixties got up and talked about how his mother had put potted plants all around her apartment—African violets, blue hydrangeas, Boston ferns. After she got sick, he would come by and water them for her. Then she died, and he continued to water the plants—he enjoyed the ritual, he said, and the plants seemed to keep her and her memory alive.

"Remember that really cold night a few weeks ago, when the electricity went out all over the city?" he asked. A number of people nodded. "The next day, I went over to my mother's house to check on the plants. They were all frozen, dead."

He paused for several seconds as he choked back tears. "It goes to show you what's absolutely necessary if you're going to stay alive in New York City in the winter," he said, with a comic's timing. "Water and a functioning electric grid." Most of the people in the room, including me, laughed along with him.

Then the man in front of me got up. He seemed nervous enough to sit back down. "I had a wand of willow," he finally said. "Potted it one winter. Hoped it'd take root in the spring." It didn't. When he reached into the soil to see if it had budded, "its white root came out in my hand." His disappointment became even more palpable as he kept searching in vain for more words.

I was beginning to understand what so many of the great Quaker thinkers had written about when they described the group dynamics of Quaker Meetings for worship. From the silence and first spoken words, a theme emerges; it resonates, takes hold, and gets internalized, until it becomes the spirit animating or speaking to the condition of the Meeting as a whole. It's not something that's preformulated or dictated from above or packaged as a pastor's sermon—it simply happens, unfolding meanings that are simultaneously ancient, current, and prophetic for people primed to listen: Sarah, for instance, who was a retired social worker.

"I think, in our Friends way, that the biggest challenge, or at least a big one, is keeping a balance between speaking truth and tenderness," she said. Sarah had clearly been inspired by the story of the fragile wand of willow. "We're truth-tellers, but how do we deliver those truths?" She let her question hang in the air for others to contemplate.

A woman in her mid-sixties got up and said, "At times I have found it necessary to lie if you want to do what's right. The poet W. H. Auden said it best, I think: 'You shall love your crooked neighbor / With your crooked heart.'"

It was the last comment of the morning. Then the woman who

served as the administrative "elder" of the Meeting stood up and shook the hand of the man next to her. Then we each shook the hands of the people next to and in front of us, ending the meeting with the Friends' traditional handshake of peace.

As Katherine and I walked home, there was a sense of calm about her. "Sarah's comment was just what I needed to put my troubles with my mom and Abigail into perspective," she said. "The need to balance truth-telling with being compassionate and effective. To be able to say things like, 'Mom, you must take your medicine and stop driving,' and 'Abigail, you must get your homework in on time,' with tenderness and love and in a way that they'll hear."

Although I didn't realize it at the time, Sarah's comment also illuminated one of my own problems. Perhaps if I talked to Ben in a less teasing, prodding way, he'd begin to see that my desire for him to play baseball wasn't predominantly selfish or Harry-esque in motivation; it was because I wanted him to experience the joy that comes with getting better and more skilled at a sport you're good at and to make the type of memories that can only come with being part of a team. Looking back, that had been my own experience playing baseball and football in high school, despite my father's zealotry.

The Act of Beginning Again

May Through September

Word had gotten out in our building: The guy in 1D was going to Quaker Meetings with the woman in 3D. No, they weren't dating, only trying on different religions. And so it came to be that Emma from 8C asked one Sunday if I wanted to accompany her to her weekly meditation group at the Union Theological Seminary, about twelve blocks north of our apartment building, on Broadway.

Emma, an ebullient, forty-something blonde, was Catholic by birth and married to a first-generation Chinese-American acupuncturist named Henry, who had grown up Buddhist. Their identical twin seven-year-old sons were ridiculously cute. And wild. So wild that my least favorite mornings of the week were Tuesday and Thursday, when it was my turn to take them to school with Noah. Those "devil" twins had no boundaries. They played chicken on the edge of the subway platform, bumped into old people without apologizing, screamed as loudly as they could when the train entered the station, jumped on seats, slid under the turnstiles, raced up the stairs and across the street without looking. Then they'd turn to say goodbye, giving you such sweet smiles you momentarily forgot all the havoc they'd just caused.

Like her sons, Emma had an exuberant personality and always knew who was who and what was what in our building. You could count on her for the latest gossip—and also to inquire after your own and your family's health. I felt genuine affection for her and was happy to accept her invitation to attend her meditation group.

The group met in a small chapel at the seminary and was led by theology professor Paul Knitter and his wife Cathy Cornell. Like the Quakers with whom I'd worshipped earlier that day, Knitter, a Buddhist-Christian, believed that compassion grew out of active listening and contemplative silence. To set the mood for the hour-long meditation, he said, "Think about a time when you felt completely safe and loved."

I closed my eyes and tried to remember a time when I felt safe, loved, and completely at ease.

I couldn't think of one.

In childhood, I felt criticized by adults who expected more from me—better grades, better behavior, fewer losses, more wins.

When I was a teenager, my father lost his job and it became my job to keep my mother from having a nervous breakdown; no one comforted me.

For years, I kept my distance from anyone who wanted to become intimate with me, which made me hard to love. When it finally happened, with Elizabeth, it was time to hurry up and have kids.

Adulthood had been a whir of taking care of business and working overtime, worrying about the kids and their futures.

I could not think of a single time when I had felt safe, nurtured, or at ease. Unless, perhaps, I counted the time I was operated on for

a herniated disc. After three months of excruciating back pain, culminating in surgery, all I could do was lie in bed on morphine while
a parade of Filipino and Dominican nurses fed me, washed me, then
tucked me in. It was heaven on earth, a vacation from my suffering.
Yet probably not what Paul Knitter was looking for.

That night, as we walked back home, I told Emma how unnerved
I'd been by Knitter's request. "My mind went blank," I said. "Then
it was filled with these horrible thoughts that kept me from meditating." Perhaps that's why I had felt so inhibited at the Morningside Meeting that morning. "I wouldn't know calm and peaceful if
I was floating in a bathtub of it."

Emma said that she knew of several people who had made meditation breakthroughs with a teacher named Sharon Salzberg. "Paul
recommends her, too," she said.

That night, I spent several minutes Googling Salzberg. Her
background was unusual for a woman who had been raised Jewish
in New York City. By the end of high school, her parents had di-
vorced, her father had abandoned her, her mother had died, she had
lived with five different families, and her father (who had come back
for a while) was put away in a mental institution.

The challenges I faced as a child were nothing compared to the
ones that dogged Salzberg.

In her sophomore year of college, she took a course in Asian
philosophy and became interested in Buddhism. On an indepen-
dent study project, she traveled to India to learn how to meditate.
The impact on her was profound, as she conveyed in an interview:
"Simply by focusing on my breath, I learned to connect fully with
my experience in a whole new way, one that enabled me to become
kinder to myself and more open to others." When she returned
home in 1974, Salzberg began teaching the techniques she had

learned in India to people with stress and chronic illness. She also cofounded the Insight Meditation Society in rural Massachusetts, which offered Buddhist meditation retreats. I saw on her website that Salzberg would be giving a workshop in New York City. I signed up.

The workshop took place at Tibet House US, a center devoted to the preservation of the Tibetan people and their culture. After leaving my shoes in the hallway, I found a cushion on the floor. Salzberg was sitting in a plush chair on a platform twenty feet in front of me. There was nothing regal about her. She wore a black sweat suit, and her short black hair framed a round, friendly face. She was leaning forward, chatting with a group of middle-aged women who were treating her like a long-lost friend.

At the start of the session, she pointed to the sculptures and paintings of Buddha in the room and said, "You don't have to be a Buddhist or a Hindu to meditate. You can meditate and still practice your own religion, or no religion at all."

Then, in her comforting cadence, she said that meditation was as easy and essential as breathing. "If you can breathe, you can meditate."

I took a deep breath, as did most of the people in the room, from the sound of it. We could breathe, we could meditate.

"On the subway. Walking down the street. Sitting at your desk. Waiting in your car. You can meditate anywhere," she said. "You can meditate when you're standing, you're sitting, you're lying down . . . and no one needs to know you're doing it."

Meditation was something anyone, at any time, could do. But lest we lose sight of its purpose, she said, "We don't meditate to get better at meditating. We meditate to get better at life. Tuning in to ourselves is just a starting point . . . for tuning in to others."

I liked Salzberg's tone and found what she said liberating. Ever since I had started meditating again, I had felt inadequate to the task. I'd get sleepier and sleepier and end up taking a nap. Or I'd get frustrated because an image of my old boss would come to mind and I couldn't get rid of it; instead, I'd keep thinking about the day he fired me. Or, out of nowhere, I'd hear a tune in my head that conjured up sad memories of old friends.

"Many distractions will arise," Salzberg said. "Thoughts, images, emotions. Aches, pains, and plans. You don't need to chase after them," she said. "Focus on your breath. Just let them go."

For me, that had always been easier said than done. My tendency had been to keep focusing on my aches and pains, or my thoughts and emotions.

"Connecting with your breath is like spotting a friend in a crowd. 'Oh, there's my friend,'" she said, as if she had just seen a friend across the room. "'Oh, there's my breath.'"

And then she gave the most useful tip of them all. She said, "The act of beginning again is the essential art of meditation practice. If you have to let go of distractions and begin again thousands of times, that's not a roadblock to the practice; that is the practice."

I began again not thousands but at least dozens of times during the following week: When I found myself falling asleep, dwelling on a thought, beating up on myself, getting interrupted by a hungry pet. I'd return to the in-breath, or, if that didn't work, I'd try meditating on the word "Sohum." They weren't fluid or restful, these meditations, but they lasted longer. I felt less frustrated. I kept on.

During the following week's class, Salzberg addressed deeper-level distractions, which she called "the add-ons." These included "foregone conclusions, rigid concepts, unexamined habits, and associative thinking." When you were meditating, you could see how much these additional layers of perception distorted your experiences, destroyed your equanimity, kept you spinning out of control.

"How do you keep the add-ons at bay while you're meditating?" one woman asked.

"You don't," Salzberg said. "You let them come and go, like passing clouds. There's no need to judge them, add to them, hold on to them, push them away. Just observe them, note them, and return to your breath."

Oh, there's my friend, I reminded myself. *Oh, there's my breath.*

That I'd get sleepy, think about my old boss, hum an old tune, or obsess about my next deadline was okay, according to Salzberg. Each of these distractions was an opportunity to investigate the thoughts, sensations, and feelings that were floating through my brain.

I gave it a try. I often felt sleepy while we meditated. I wanted to yawn; usually I'd suppress my desire to do it. But this time, I indulged it. I yawned. And, while I was yawning, I realized how depressed I'd been feeling. My typical way of responding to that realization would have been to obsess on the ten or fifteen reasons I felt depressed. This time, I simply took note of how I felt: *I'm depressed.* Then I returned to my breath. *Oh, there's my breath.* I could deal with the reasons for my depression later; for now, I was glad to be feeling more peaceful and refreshed.

Salzberg devoted the third session to metta meditation. Unlike vipassana, or "insight," meditation, which was about becoming more mindful and present in the moment, metta aimed to cultivate compassion for ourselves, for others, and for every sentient being.

She started by instructing us to sit quietly and say the following words to ourselves:

> May I be safe,
> May I be happy,
> May I be healthy, ·
> May I live with ease.

By saying those words, we were acknowledging how vulnerable we were to change and suffering, the human condition. Once we were able to focus "caring attention" on ourselves, we could extend that same quality of attention to others.

She asked us to think of someone close to us, someone in need, and to say:

> May you be safe,
> May you be happy,
> May you be healthy,
> May you live with ease.

My friend Liz came to mind. For the past two years, she had been undergoing a painful regimen of chemotherapy. It wasn't hard for me to direct those words with all my heart toward Liz—I loved her and she was suffering. Nor was it hard for me to direct those words to Emma and her twins. They might annoy me at times, but they also made me smile. And I wanted Emma to be less overwhelmed by stress, and the twins to be kept safe in the subways.

But when Salzberg asked us to focus our attention on someone we didn't know well—for example, the cashier at the local supermarket—it was harder for me to feel authentic and caring. To establish an emotional connection, I tried to picture the real-life cashier at my corner supermarket smiling at me as I paid for my groceries. Then I tried to imagine that her husband had died. Because the act of inventing this sad incident was contrived, I had trouble saying the metta meditation for the cashier with any genuine compassion or enthusiasm.

Salzberg asked us to focus caring attention on someone who was difficult: I chose my old boss. It was really, really hard for me to generate goodwill toward him. My metta couldn't withstand the lingering ill will I felt toward him, even five years after he had fired me.

Metta is also known as loving-kindness meditation. "It cultivates the ability to see the humanity in people we don't know and the pain in people we find difficult," Salzberg said. As much as I had been trying to see "that which is God" in everyone, I clearly had a long way to go.

By this time it was summer, and I began to make a concerted effort to use Salzberg's meditation techniques as I sat in silence at Quaker meetings. If I got antsy or overly distracted, I'd note what I was feeling and return to my breath. If I started thinking harsh thoughts, I'd do a loving-kindness meditation, widening my circle of compassion from myself . . . to someone I loved . . . to someone who bothered me . . . to every sentient being.

During one meeting, the person who was bothering me was sitting right behind me. A woman had brought her seven-month-old daughter, and all through the hour of silence Maggie kept screaming, "Baa, baa, baa," as if she were a newborn lamb. Each time she

did that, I winced. I even winced in the moments between the bleat-
ing noises, in anticipation of them. I thought about turning around
and telling Maggie's mother to quiet her down or take her outside,
but that would have been poor etiquette and gone against the spirit
of the meeting. I tried a loving-kindness meditation—*May you be
safe, may you be happy*, and so on—to Maggie, but she drowned it
out. And then an unbidden image of Ben and Caroline suddenly
came to mind, causing me to remember when my children were
her age.

"This is the time in our meeting when we ask if anyone has any
joys and concerns they'd like to share," a woman said.

I stood up and looked back at Maggie and her mother. Then I
talked for the first time ever in nearly eight months of meetings. I
said, "Maggie helped me see a simultaneous joy and concern and
also a need. The joy was the feeling I got when my children were her
age and they looked to me and my wife to quiet their fears and sing
them to sleep." Those early years of parenting were the sweetest of
our marriage. Our small family unit was a world unto itself, defined
by the needs and whims of our children, who were dependent exclusively on us. "Now that my kids are teenagers, they don't want to
be around us during their free time; they'd rather be out with their
friends. Maggie helped me realize how much I miss that period of
my children's life—and how I need to find a new joy in parenting as
my children assert their freedom to grow up."

I wasn't in town for the meeting that took place on the tenth
anniversary of the World Trade Center tragedy, but I was there a
week later, on September 18, when twenty-six people gathered in
the tower of Riverside Church to mind the Light.

When the hour was almost over, the woman next to me stood up
and said, "I may never experience silence again. However, today I

was able to experience quiet. Thank you." I wasn't sure what she meant. I later learned that four years earlier the woman had been attacked, beaten, and left for dead. She lay for weeks in a coma. Then a sentence went through her head: I will not make that man a murderer. She didn't: She woke up from her coma. Hence, her gratitude for this morning's quiet, and her sober recognition that she might never experience the serenity that we were striving for in this room again.

Ned, the other person who spoke, was wearing a hooded black sweatshirt that made him look like a monk. His frail hands held what looked to be an intravenous fluid bag. He got up slowly to speak. He began by listing several "isms"—theism, materialism, socialism, capitalism. Then, in what I can best describe as a thunderous whisper, he said, "There is no Quakerism in this room. Instead, it's mysticism we experience here—mysticism!—that sense of something sudden, inexplicable, beyond what any of us can understand."

I wasn't sure what was motivating Ned to say that, or what he meant. Then he told us what had happened to him a week earlier, on the tenth anniversary of 9/11, how he had looked down and seen a puddle of water on the floor in front of him, how his right shirtsleeve was all wet, how liquid seemed to be flowing from his forearm.

"It wasn't sweat," he told us. "It was this damn intravenous contraption leaking all the medications that were keeping me alive."

Ned called 911 and told the woman who answered that he had been waiting for a heart transplant for over a year, that the fluid had all leaked out, that if they didn't come right away and get him to the hospital he'd become dehydrated and maybe die.

"You can imagine how I felt when she told me that EMTs

couldn't come because the streets were closed off from a 9/11-related bomb threat," he said. "I was really pissed off. But I stayed put. Then, maybe ten minutes later, I called 911 again."

This time the woman told Ned to take the subway to the hospital. He told her that, given his condition, there was absolutely no way he could make it there. She put him on hold to take another call. "Then something, a voice inside, told me to get up and try to get to the subway anyway. And I did," he said. "I got to the subway and to the hospital. And when I got there they took my blood pressure. It was fifty over thirty-three, the blood pressure of someone who was about to be dead."

That's why Ned was saying that there wasn't Quakerism but mysticism in the room—the presence within and around us of something so much greater than us that sustains us with timely guidance, so long as we listen for it in the quiet of our hearts.

It was incredible how, at every meeting I had attended over the last eight months, at least one person told a miraculous story like that.

"Wow!" Katherine said as we walked down Riverside Drive toward our apartment building. "What Ned said just blew me away."

"Blew me away, too," I said.

Then Katherine told me about her own mystical experience. It had happened the same day Ned heard the voice and made his way to the subway and the hospital. Katherine was standing on the steps of the Firemen's Memorial in Riverside Park, where dozens of our neighbors were gathered to commemorate the 343 firefighters and paramedics who had died on 9/11. "I got really emotional and tripped as I was getting down," she recalled. "But before I could get hurt, the crowd lifted me by my elbows and steadied me.

"We're so damn vulnerable," Katherine added. "We're always

tripping, stumbling, and falling down. But isn't that the reason we're all here: to lift each other up, to keep each other from getting hurt?"

It was a stunning sentiment—and one I believed. We're here to lift each other up, easing each other's pain and suffering.

Buddha Body, Buddha Mind

October Through November

For my fifty-eighth birthday Elizabeth presented me with a statue of a meditating Buddha. She had gotten it at Brimfield, the giant flea market in western Massachusetts. "I thought it might inspire you," she said. "The woman who sold it to me said that it was carved in Bali, from volcanic stone, and painted saffron, the traditional color of Buddhist monks. Like it?"

I did. Everything about this Buddha was serene—his closed eyes, his soft smile, his only slightly dipped chin. He was sitting in a half-lotus position, with his right foot on his left thigh. And his hands, resting on his lap, were in the classic dhyana mudra position—palms up, with his right hand cradled in his left. This was said to be the way the Buddha was sitting in the moments before he attained enlightenment under the Bodhi tree.

I also liked Elizabeth's gift because it reinforced my sense that it was time for me to begin exploring another contemplative tradition. From the Quakers, I had experienced the spiritual power of sitting in expectant silence and looking within. From Sharon Salzberg, I had gotten a taste of Buddhist meditation techniques and a sense of how Buddhism might help me cultivate a more compassionate attitude. Now, in the presence of Buddha's statue, I felt compelled to find out more about the great spiritual master's life and to see what perspective it might offer on my midlife quest. I began by reading Karen Armstrong's *Buddha*, part of the Penguin Lives series. I also reread the Buddhism section of Huston Smith's *The Religions of Man*, a book I had first read in high school.

As I went back and forth between the two books, I found myself increasingly troubled by the turning point in Buddha's life: his decision, at age twenty-nine, to abandon his young family and retreat into the forest in search of spiritual enlightenment. When I was in high school, I cheered him on without any feeling for how his actions would impact the people who loved and relied on him. Now, at age fifty-eight, my emotions were complicated by the fact that I had a wife and three young children who depended on me.

Before he became the Buddha, his name was Siddhartha Gautama. He was born in Lumbini, a town in present-day Nepal, around 560 B.C., to an aristocrat named Suddhodana and his wife, Maya, who died a week after giving birth to him. (Siddhartha was raised by his aunt, Mahapajapati, who married Suddhodana in her sister's place.) An assembly of fortune-tellers told Suddhodana that Siddhartha would grow up to be either a powerful king or a great sage. Suddhodana did everything he could to keep Siddhartha on the king track. That meant shielding him from the world's ills so that he wouldn't feel compelled to either renounce the world or save it.

Siddhartha grew up in three luxurious palaces. Each time he'd leave them, his bodyguards would sweep the streets clean of anything that might blemish his fairy-tale view of life. When he was sixteen, he married a neighboring princess named Yasodhara; she bore him a son they named Rahula. Siddhartha and his family remained ignorant of all suffering—both the world's and their own.

One day, as he rode in his chariot, Siddhartha looked out the window and saw a bent-over old man the guards had missed. In this unexpected way, he encountered the horrifying reality of aging.

On subsequent rides he came upon a man who was sick, and then a corpse, exposing him to illness and the fact that all men die. Then, on his fourth eye-opening ride, he saw a robed monk with a shaved head. Now he knew that it was possible to withdraw from the world: his father's worst nightmare.

From then on, it became impossible for Siddhartha to enjoy the worldly pleasures around him. As Armstrong put it, "The veil that had concealed life's pain had been torn aside and the universe seemed a prison of pain and pointlessness." In secret, Siddhartha shaved his head and donned the clothes of a beggar. Then he disappeared into the forest for what would become a six-year search for enlightenment.

As a teenager I wanted to emulate Siddhartha; now, as I was about to "go forth" on my own spiritual adventure, I wasn't sure. When my three children were born, I experienced an abundance of love, joy, and gratitude that was beyond anything I ever could have imagined. Siddhartha, on the other hand, was disgusted when Rahula was born. As a father, you want your children to grow up with confidence that they are deeply loved. That was one of the main reasons I chose to conduct my spiritual search within two hours of my home. Siddhartha had abandoned his wife and son in the middle of the night with nary a goodbye. Why?

According to Armstrong, Siddhartha realized that family life would create a level of attachment, obligation, and longing that would cause him endless suffering. For that reason, she wrote, it would be "incompatible with the highest forms of spirituality." Siddhartha wasn't the only great religious figure who came to this conclusion. Centuries later, Jesus would say, "If any man come to me, and not hate his father and mother, wife and children and brethren and sisters, yea and his own life also, he cannot be my disciple."

Didn't God—or at least the God of Moses—tell us to honor our fathers and mothers?

Not always, it seemed. In order to become a true disciple and achieve your highest spiritual potential, Jesus said that you must undergo a total shift of consciousness—you must be reborn. To do that, you need to reject everything that constituted your old life, leaving your old self and identity behind.

And that's what Siddhartha did. He stripped off his previous life. Then he joined the hordes of bhikkus, or renunciants, who were wandering around northern India at the time. Like them, he was looking for a teacher who had a dharma (doctrine) and sangha (community of disciples) that could hasten his path to enlightenment. There were dozens to choose from.

At first Siddhartha was drawn to a group of ascetics who sought enlightenment through punishing periods of fasting and self-denial. It took him two years to conclude that this ascetic approach was just as limiting as the hedonistic path to happiness he had followed as a youth. Instead, he began following what he called the "Middle Way." Through the practice of yoga, meditation, and various mindfulness techniques, he became increasingly skillful at controlling his ego-centered desires and delusions. He became wiser and more compassionate. He learned to act nonviolently, with loving-kindness toward all.

Six years after setting out on his journey, Siddhartha found his way to an ancient fig tree near Gaya, a town just south of the city of Patna. It was there that he achieved enlightenment and became Buddha—the "Awakened One." His great realization, according to Armstrong, was that all sentient beings are "inherently complete and perfect. But they do not realize it because of their delusions and cravings." After extinguishing the fires of greed, hatred, and ignorance in himself, Buddha could have just kept sitting under the Bodhi tree, enjoying his hard-earned enlightenment. Instead, he decided to help others achieve enlightenment. For nearly forty-five years, until his death at the age of eighty, he wandered the streets and deer parks of northern India preaching what Smith calls "the ego-shattering, life-redeeming elixir of his message."

It made me happy to hear that Yasodhara, Rahula, and Mahapajapati eventually became members of his sangha. (Although it's important to note that, true to his Buddha nature, the man formerly known as Siddhartha didn't treat his family in any special way.) But my main takeaway from Smith's and Armstrong's books was Buddhism's distrust of creed and ritual—and Buddha's emphasis on the qualities of compassion, loving-kindness, and peace. These were many of the same qualities that had drawn me to Quakerism.

Buddha famously said, "Do not accept what you hear by report, do not accept tradition, do not accept a statement because it is found in your books, nor because it is in accord with your belief . . . nor because it is the saying of your teacher. . . . Be ye lamps unto yourselves."

Like the Quakers, Buddha believed in the power and authority of direct personal experience. Quakers, for the most part, believe that the Light Within emanates from God, whereas Buddha warned that a reliance on anything supernatural—for example, God—could keep a person from becoming skillful enough spiritually to achieve enlightenment. Whatever their differences, Buddhism and Quakerism are similar in this one important regard: They aren't for shirkers or fatalists; they are for people who are willing to work hard spiritually and assume responsibility for their own actions and fate.

For the past thirty years I had been living in the most competitive, materialistic, and power-hungry city on earth. I had been working in a profession that valued scoops, aggressiveness, and meeting deadlines. I had been living on the edge, caught in a cycle of pushing myself until I felt too burned out to go on. I'd periodically get sick from all the stress. Then, as soon as I was feeling better, I'd forget how stressed out and miserable I'd been and hop back up on the relentlessly turning wheel.

It was a crazy way to live, full of highs and lows and angst and pitfalls. Buddha talked about a Middle Way that could lead to self-healing and enlightenment. I wanted to learn more what Buddha meant by that—and whether it might be a path for me to follow.

I was back at Tibet House meditating, but the disembodied voice that told us to close our eyes and to "unplug" our awareness from "the many plans, worries, and activities that dissipate our energies and complicate our lives" did not come from the calmly reassuring Sharon Salzberg. It came from a man with an intense, probing, even intellectual timbre to his voice. Perhaps wrongly, I presumed he was trying to challenge me and the dozens of other meditators who were gathered there.

"How do you feel being in your living body right now?" he asked us.

My living body? As opposed to what—my dead one? I was tempted to say.

But then I remembered what Salzberg had said about using your add-ons—in this case, my bias against the quality of the man's voice—as an opportunity to investigate your thoughts, emotions, and sensations. When I did that, I was aware of the cold metal chair I was sitting in, how much my thighs ached, how I was so itchy I could jump out of my skin.

"Imagine the world as a place of clarity and calm, energy and awareness," he said, guiding us deeper into meditation.

I tried to imagine a large orb radiating energy and calm.

"Breathe it all in," he said. "Breathe in the city, the planet, the solar system. Feel that you are a world in a grain of sand."

It was a reference to William Blake's "Auguries of Innocence." We had learned it in high school: "To see a world in a grain of sand / And a heaven in a wild flower / Hold infinity in the palm of your hand / And eternity in an hour." I had recited that poem to dozens of girls and women over the years, including my wife.

"Now picture yourself as a bubble of life," the voice said, "floating in equilibrium, in allostasis, with all the other living bubbles in the world."

I didn't know what "allostasis" meant. So I kept chewing on the word—"al-lo-stasis, allo-stasis, allostas-is"—like a dog with a bone.

It was time for me to find my breath: Oh, there's my friend. Oh, there's my breath. But as soon as I found it I became aware that I couldn't breathe through my left nostril, the result of a football injury that had shattered my nose and deviated my septum more than forty years ago. Instead of anchoring me in the present, my breath had carried me back to one of the most traumatic moments in my past. For some reason, perhaps because I was getting over a cold, I was more aware of my clogged and deviated septum than usual.

"Now slowly open your eyes. . . ."

I looked around the room. There were maybe fifty people sitting on metal chairs and meditation cushions. It was a downtown crowd: college students, young hipsters, women with lithe yoga bodies. There were some older hipsters, too: bald men in black T-shirts, women wearing saris and the type of hippie garb you could buy at any street fair.

The voice that had been guiding us belonged to a thin, white-haired man who was wearing a black turtleneck and beret. He sat on the platform in a comfy reading chair. His legs were crossed at the ankles. And whenever his voice got hoarse, he sipped from a cup of tea.

Joe Loizzo is a Harvard-trained psychiatrist and Columbia-trained Buddhist scholar who had spent more than thirty years studying the beneficial effects of meditation on healing and learning. At Columbia, he had studied with Bob Thurman, a former Buddhist monk who was a leading expert on Tibetan Buddhism and culture. Then, in 1998, Loizzo founded the Nalanda Institute for Contemplative Science in Manhattan, which was loosely affiliated with Tibet House. His inspiration had been Nalanda University in Bihar, India, which was founded in the fifth century B.C. to advance Buddha's mission of ending human suffering.

I realized that Loizzo wasn't anywhere near as challenging as my imagination had made him out to be; he was rather accommodating. "Please, make yourself comfortable," he said to the latecomers. "I see two seats in the back, a few here. There are several meditation pillows . . . here, here, and here . . . and one right here in front of me."

As I had come to understand it, there were two main schools of Buddhist thought: Theravada and Mahayana. Theravada says that you have to be a monk or religious professional to become enlightened. Mahayana believes that the path of enlightenment is also open to laypeople. The goal in Theravada is to become an arhat, a perfected being; in Mahayana it is to become a bodhisattva, a person who delays his or her own enlightenment to help others lead a more contemplative and happy life.

No wonder Belief-O-Matic had listed Mahayana Buddhism as one of the top five religions I should explore—and that I had ended up here, at Nalanda, taking a course called "Foundations of Self-Healing and the Contemplative Life," from a bodhisattva named Joe.

Loizzo explained that the text for the course would be Buddha's Four Noble Truths, the conceptual framework for all Buddhist thought. The version we'd be reading had been translated from Pali into English by Geshe Tashi Tsering, a Tibetan Buddhist monk and scholar who lives in London. "We'll also be practicing meditation and mindfulness," he said. "And you'll be learning how to integrate Buddhist precepts like right speech, right action, and right behavior into your lives."

Loizzo's stop-and-go delivery brought the comedian Woody Allen to mind. Both men tended to digress a lot and muse at their own self-deprecating jokes, even as they obsessed about the woeful nature of the human condition. But whereas Woody went to psychiatrists, Loizzo was one. And he considered Buddha, who lived more than twenty-five hundred years ago, an even more important scientist and healer than Freud. "The Four Noble Truths are no less than an owner's manual for dealing with human suffering," he said. "Follow them step-by-step and you'll get results."

Before sending us out into the chill October night, Loizzo led us through a brief meditation. He instructed us to close our eyes and look within ourselves. "Become scientists and also therapists of your own bodies and minds," he said. "Where there's fatigue, breathe life. Where there's numbness, breathe in energy. Now tune in to your mind's natural purity, to its spaciousness and plasticity," he said softly. "It is here that you'll find equanimity and peace—and the happiness that you and all sentient beings seek."

It had been a strange first class for me. My mind had flitted all over the place and I had begun by feeling challenged by Loizzo. And yet, by the end of the class, I had come to genuinely like him: He knew his stuff, and it was clear that he wanted to help us turn our suffering into happiness.

When I got home, Elizabeth was lying on the couch in her gray robe and lucky red socks, reading a client's manuscript while listening to the last Detroit Tigers game of the season. (They were playing the Baltimore Orioles.) The kids were in bed, the Tigers were ahead, and Elizabeth was surrounded by her dogs (on the floor) and her cats (by her head): heaven.

"So how was it?" she finally asked, during the seventh-inning stretch.

"Fine," I said.

"Any cute women there try to pick you up?"

That was always Elizabeth's playful first question whenever I came back from a class or spiritual retreat. Because she knew that an unattached man at these sorts of events was a rarity, she was glad that I was wearing my wedding ring.

I knew she was kidding. But still, I took the Fifth. Otherwise, I would have needed to confess that I had noticed several attractive women that night, especially when I was bored. In that sense, several women did pick me up: They picked up my flagging energy and had an unintended espresso-jolt effect on me.

"Go, Orioles," I said slyly beneath my breath.

That night I started reading Tsering's translation. In his introduction to the text, he referred to the Four Noble Truths as Buddha's "first and most essential teaching." The truths are:

    I. The Noble Truth of Suffering
    II. The Noble Truth of the Origin of Suffering
    III. The Noble Truth of the Cessation of Suffering
    IV. The Noble Truth of the Path to the Cessation of Suffering

Forty-nine days after his enlightenment, Buddha revealed these four truths to the five ascetics who had accompanied him during his years of wandering. Why did Buddha detail the nature of suffering before its causes? Because that's how he had gained his knowledge of the first two truths. First he had become aware of the fact that we age, get sick, and die; then he resolved to "fix" the suffering we experienced as a result of these conditions. The same was true of the third and fourth truths. Once he understood the fact that there could be an end to suffering, he could put forth a step-by-step program for ending it. As it said in the text:

Everything is made of Causes,
And the Transcendent One taught those Causes,
And how to master them.
Such was his way.

Before I arrived at the second class, I decided to do something I never did: sit in the front row. That way I could focus my full attention on Loizzo's explanation of Buddha's First Noble Truth, without the distractions of pretty women or anything else.

"We get hungry and sick," he began. "We age and die. Even the gods, in their Jacuzzis, start decaying in the end."

I loved that line. It conjured up Charles Foster Kane, Jay Gatsby, and Bernie Madoff for me. The rich and famous may think they're immune to suffering. But in the end, they, too, get old, sick, and die.

The week before, I had found myself focused on externals: the fact that Loizzo sounded like Woody Allen and was attired in Beat generation black. But now, listening to him from just a few feet away, I was mainly aware of the compassion in his voice: "There's the-grass-is-always-greener sort of suffering," he said. "And the suffering of loss we feel when a friend dies, or a wonderful experience comes to an end. There's the disappointment we feel when things aren't what we wanted or expected them to be. And there's spiritual or existential suffering—the sort that leads us to question our very existence and the purpose of our lives."

As he was talking, I found myself thinking about my own litany of suffering. It started with my first memory: the humiliation I experienced when my nursery school teacher made me take off my pants in front of my whole class because I'd peed in them. It was my first day of school, and I'd been too embarrassed to do what she had requested: "Raise your hand if you need to go to the bathroom." I didn't. So she made an example of me.

There was the pain and disappointment I felt when I threw out my arm and was forced to realize that my dream of playing college baseball was over. And the insecurities that surfaced when I was rejected by girls and women I had ached for and employers who either fired or didn't hire me.

There was the almost unbearable sadness I felt when my high school girlfriend was killed in a car crash, when we buried my four grandparents, when so many of my friends and loved ones were dying of AIDS, cancer, and depression, too often by their own trembling hands.

And there was the sadness I now felt whenever Ben, Noah, and Caroline turned away from my hugs and kisses in public.

The truth was, scrutinized closely enough, everything I had longed for and striven for and clung to—everything I had said, dreamt, and done; even my marriage, with its spiritual strife—had produced its own measure of suffering, as such situations and longings had for the entire human race. And now I could add rashes, age spots, and wrinkles on my skin to the list, and say, with Prufrock, "I grow old . . . I grow old . . . I shall wear the bottom of my trousers rolled."

"We suffer when bad things happen to good people and we can't figure out why," Loizzo was saying. I thought about the eight-year-old girl who had been killed earlier that day in the Bronx in a drive-by shooting: She could have been my daughter, or the girl next door.

Loizzo then said, "We convince ourselves that there shouldn't be terrorists, even though we know that there are people in the world who are pissed off and want to kill us because they are hungry and don't have jobs, and because they have so much less than we do, with no prospects ahead." I had not lived with that level of starvation and desperation. But it wasn't hard for me to understand the terrorists and their rage: I could extrapolate it from my own anger at the disparities in the world, and my own hunger for respect.

We cry when we are born. And we continue crying—from the pain, the heartbreak, the uniquely human knowledge that we will die and return to dust. To live means to suffer: With regard to the First Noble Truth, Buddha and I were on the same page.

I wasn't so sure about the Second Noble Truth. Each time I read it, I became more confused. In breaking down the causes of suffering, Buddha made distinctions between contaminated and uncontaminated intentions, the five afflictive emotions, and the twelve links of dependent origination. Those sorts of abstractions (and technical-sounding words) gave me a huge headache. I was hoping that Loizzo would shed light on this dense material in his next class. Thank Buddha, he did.

"Parents who abuse their children cause terrible trauma," he said. "But even the good mom leaves her baby in the bassinet, with the baby left wondering if she'll ever come back. And we carry that memory forward in our lives."

That made sense to me; it really did. I could picture a baby screaming in terror because it felt abandoned. I could see how childhood traumas (for example, peeing in your pants, or losing a favorite pet) could lead to the psychological and emotional suffering we experience as adults.

"We live in the story of the world we made up when we were three years old—when we were small, unable to care for ourselves, and everyone else was either a god or a demon based on whether they helped or hurt us," Loizzo said. "In the Buddhist view, narcissism is the worst disease we humans have. It is very self-gratifying to think we're the only beings that matter. But it means living the fantasy and not the reality of who we are." Why was living that way so bad? "If you can't tune in to who you really are, you can't acknowledge the existence of anyone who disagrees with you. Nor can you genuinely care about another person. You end up isolated, on guard, prone to constant and debilitating stress."

According to Loizzo, each of the Four Noble Truths corresponds to a particular "scope" of mindfulness. For instance, the Noble Truth of Suffering corresponds to the human body, which manifests suffering through aches and pains and changes in the nervous system. During the opening and closing meditations for the class on that noble truth, Loizzo led us to become more mindful of our bodies. During one such meditation, he asked us to notice how often we grit our teeth and tighten our shoulders when we feel stressed. I responded to his question by clenching my jaw, gritting my teeth, and hunching forward, which caused my shoulders to squinch up. It was interesting to see how my anticipatory stress about meditating on my body's stress had caused my body to get even more stressed out.

To help us deal more skillfully with our body's stress response, Loizzo urged us to accept the inescapable reality that we are fated to die: poof, finis, like every other being, sentient or not. When he said that, I found myself getting sad and then combative. I tightened the muscles of my neck and upper back and readied myself to rage against the dying of the light. But Loizzo had a good point: If we're going to die, why cling so fiercely to our aging bodies or to any fantasy we have that we're going to exist forever? Instead, he said, "Breathe into your body and gently ponder its purpose. Ask yourself, How would I like to use this body in the brief time I will be inhabiting it?" My jaws and shoulders relaxed.

The current class—on the Noble Truth of the Origin of Suffering—had shown us how we suffer because we continue to tell ourselves the story of the world we made up when we were frightened, vulnerable three-year-olds. The scope corresponding to the Second Noble Truth involved our sensations. How could we relate to them in a way that made us less compulsive and driven? And, beyond that, how could we envision an alternative reality that was more consistent with who we actually are and would like to be? "Imagine a place where everything you think or do makes you feel more secure, profound, energetic, at peace," Loizzo said. Then he posed a riddle: "What are you left with when you take away the worry, frustration, and confusion from your life?"

Fewer wrinkles? Tighter abs? A good night's sleep? I mused to myself.

"Buddha body, Buddha mind," he said.

I had to presume that Buddha had the same human brain as everyone else. So what did my brain—and Buddha's—look like? And how did it work?

On Loizzo's recommendation, I spent an afternoon at the American Museum of Natural History, taking in an exhibit called "Brain: The Inside Story." En route, I strolled through halls filled with dinosaur fossils and dioramas displaying stuffed birds and animals in their natural habitats. The brain exhibit literally lit me up: An artist had draped the hallway with fifteen hundred pounds of recycled wire, illuminated by strobes and beams of light, creating a corridor of firing neuronal networks.

I wasn't a total dunce about the brain. I knew, for instance, that it has evolved over millions of years. That it uses molecular, chemical, and electrical signals, traveling up and down the spinal cord, to get us to breathe, move, and interact with our surroundings. That there are specific areas of the brain devoted to seeing, hearing, tasting, smelling, and touching. That, like parts in an orchestra, these different areas communicate with each other to convey the full richness of whatever we are experiencing.

Here's what I didn't know about the three-pound lump of gray matter called the human brain: It contains a hundred billion neurons. (I repeat: a hundred billion of them.) Each neuron can connect to a thousand other neurons and send out as many as a thousand electrochemical signals per second—at a speed of 250 miles per hour. Those facts blew my mind. As did evolution's method for building the brain layer by layer over those millions of years.

First came the lizard or reptile brain, which we inherited from lizards and fish. It is responsible for functions like breathing, coordination, balance, feeding, mating, and defense.

The limbic system, or mammal brain, came next; it governs our emotions.

The cortex, or primate brain, came last. It enables us to remember the past and imagine the future so that we are uniquely able to plan, make decisions, and communicate with each other by language.

You could get a sense of the brain's audacious architecture by walking around the gigantic bulbous sculpture of the cortical brain that occupied one of the exhibition halls. As a recorded voice explained how the brain helps us reason, remember, and use language, the areas responsible for these functions lit up, reflecting the increased blood flow to these areas when they are active.

Another display put you in the brain of a London taxicab driver as he navigated that city's complex warren of streets. Longtime London cabbies have a larger than average hippocampus, the area responsible for creating long-term memories.

In the final room of the exhibit, called the Brain Lounge, you could sit on gray couches shaped like brain matter and see fMRIs showing the blood flow to specific regions in the brains of various high achievers—for example, the cellist Yo-Yo Ma and the basketball player Landry Fields—as they talked about why they're successful at what they do.

But my favorite part of the exhibit was the one that showed some of the tricks the brain can play as it shapes your perceptions of what you're experiencing. Looking at an image of pouring rain, I interpreted the accompanying sound as that of rain falling; in actuality, it was the sound of bacon sizzling that I was hearing.

Loizzo's next class was focused on how traumatic memories and worst-case thinking undermine our evolutionary instinct for happiness.

"It starts in the amygdala," he said, which made me glad to have gone to the brain exhibit, which had taught me that the amygdala houses the fight-or-flight response that helped our prehistoric ancestors survive in the wild.

When the amygdala perceives a threat, it triggers our body's stress response. Loizzo explained what happens: "Our pulse rate goes up. Our blood pressure goes up. The pituitary gland releases steroids, adrenaline—it puts out endorphins, too." In effect, we get hijacked by stress. It shuts down the part of our brain that houses our intelligence, creativity, and people skills, so we're left with only our primal instinct to fight or run away. "That worked brilliantly against hyenas, wolves, and saber-toothed tigers," Loizzo said. But today's threats come mainly from our spouses, bosses, colleagues, and business rivals: "We end up treating them like predators."

The real damage occurs later. That's because the chemicals that are released in response to the perceived threat stay in our bodies for as many as six hours. Say the boss dresses us down or gives us short shrift. "Since we can't fight the boss," Loizzo said, "we get all worked up and stew in our cubicle all day. Or we take out our frustrations on our wives and kids. Or we disassociate ourselves from reality—and retreat into fantasies of grandiosity and revenge."

Sound familiar?

"We're the luckiest people on the planet," Loizzo concluded. "And yet, we don't feel good about either what we have or who we are. Instead, with our nervous systems still hovering in trauma, we go around feeling like frightened animals."

That night, I couldn't stop thinking about all the people I had known who had let never-ending cycles of stress and trauma poison their lives and devour their chances for happiness.

My mother, for example, whose irrational fears of becoming a bag lady rendered her useless and even belligerent whenever our family faced a financial challenge. My father, whose stubborn fear of breaking the rules kept him from ever taking a risk.

My wealthy Nana Shirley, who had been born into poverty, kept her silver and antiques under lock and key, afraid that other people would steal them; she never experienced the pleasure of simply enjoying them. My friend Jake, whose parents had nearly starved to death in Nazi concentration camps, couldn't order a meal in a restaurant without finding fault with the food and sending it back.

It was easier for some of my addict friends to weather the highs and lows of substance abuse than to get off drugs and face the emptiness they felt inside. I was not an addict, but I had let my fears and compulsive behavior keep me from loving and being loved and from feeling as fulfilled as I might have been at work.

What Loizzo had said about the luckiest people on the planet hit home. I was certainly one of the lucky ones. But I didn't feel good about what I had or who I was, even with my abundance of blessings. Was it because of the story of the world I kept telling myself, the story I had made up when I was three? The people in that story humiliated me in public and screamed at each other so loudly at the dinner table that I'd eat and eat and eat just to shut out their voices. Even after they disappointed and wronged me, the people in that story commanded me to give them a good night kiss.

It was a story steeped in fear, shame, and love-on-demand, in never being good enough and deserving only to suffer. I had been telling myself that story all my life—and, in so doing, I had continued to shoulder the burdens of that world. It didn't need to be that way, according to Loizzo. We can tell ourselves a different story, one that helps us act on our other fundamental human instinct: the instinct for happiness.

Again, he pointed to recent studies that had proven the plasticity of the human brain. When I was growing up in the 1960s, scientists believed that the brain stopped growing in early adulthood. But with recent advances in neuroscience we now know that the brain creates new neural pathways and alters existing ones throughout life, particularly as it adapts to new experiences and learns new information (or as we begin to tell ourselves a more positive story about our lives).

"Studies show that people who have positive emotions—and act in positive ways—experience a higher level of well-being," Loizzo added. He ticked off the emotions of love, compassion, tolerance, bliss, curiosity, hope, gratitude, euphoria, self-confidence, sympathy, generosity, and equanimity. "These positive emotions are part of our medicine. We need to take them in high doses."

Telling ourselves a story that reflects our aspirations for a joyous, fulfilling life is part of that process. So is ridding our mind of the delusions, cravings, and attachments that poison it. "The Buddha says that by mastering our nervous systems we can transform our stressful moments into nonevents," Loizzo said. "We can't eliminate all the stressors in our lives. But we can unlearn our habits for reacting to stressful moments in ways that steep us in stress."

The Second Noble Truth was starting to make more sense to me.

I had a strange dream that night. I was in the desert, in a war zone. I had brought way too much stuff along—golf clubs, weights, boxes of old tennis shoes. I had to sort it all out before the generals came. Running out of time, I swept some of my stuff into a hole, then covered it with sand.

When I looked up, several Marines were running through an obstacle course headed straight for me. My first response was, They're going to kill someone—me? I felt pressured to shoot but it was so chaotic that I couldn't tell my enemies from my friends. I was mostly aware of wanting to go back home with only one suitcase.

When I woke up, I realized what the dream was trying to tell me: I needed to get rid of the unnecessary stress and suffering in my life so that I could travel through life with more clarity and ease.

Also, I needed to pack for my trip to Cleveland.

I was scheduled to fly to various cities in Michigan and Florida to promote my book *Unfinished Business*. Along the way I planned to do what I had done on November 4 the previous two years: visit my Aunt Fern on her birthday. I flew to Cleveland early that morning, so I could drive out to the special-care facility by noon. When I got there, Fern's wheelchair was parked in its usual place, in a corner by the nurses' desk. When I lifted her head to kiss her, I could see that something was wrong. She had tubes in her nostrils, and her arms and legs were badly bruised. Also, it took longer than usual for her to recognize me.

"Is that you, Lee Richard?" she finally asked.

"Of course," I said. "Don't I always come here to celebrate your birthday with you?"

She glanced up but didn't say anything.

"How does it feel to be sixty-nine?" I asked.

"Sixty-nine? I'm sixty-nine?" she said incredulously. She looked scared. "I feel terrible, Lee Richard, terrible. My roommate tried to kill me last night. She put a pillow on my head. I can't breathe anymore. The doctor stuck all these needles in me. Look how black-and-blue and swollen I am." She held out her arms and legs for me to see. "You have to get me out of here before they kill me," she pleaded. "Help me, Lee Richard."

I rubbed her back to comfort her. On my previous visits I could hum an old show tune she liked—for example, "I Feel Pretty" from *West Side Story* or "What Do the Simple Folk Do?" from *Camelot*—and she'd calm down. Or I could wheel her into the courtyard for a cigarette. But ever since she'd had pneumonia a few months earlier, she had been forbidden to smoke. So I wheeled her into the front lobby. There, in a quiet corner, away from the muttering and dozing Alzheimer's patients, I could set up my computer and present Fern with her birthday gift: a slide show of the twins' b'nai mitzvah.

On previous birthdays I'd given her a Jewish wall calendar, two CDs of Jewish holiday music, and a scrapbook of photos from a trip she had taken to Israel with my grandparents when she was nine. Fern cared deeply about being Jewish. But, as she told me, "I'm the only Jewish person living here, the only one, and it's hard for me to keep the Sabbath and Jewish holidays." I had asked her social worker to arrange occasional visits from a local rabbi. Now, on her birthday, I hoped to give her a vicarious experience of the twins' Jewish rite of passage.

"Your niece and nephew would have loved for you to be there," I said, as a photo of Ben and Caroline appeared on the screen. "You would have been very proud of them."

"Proud," she said listlessly. "I would have been proud."

The next photo showed Ben reading from the Torah. "Doesn't he look handsome?" I asked.

I could barely hear Fern's answer of yes. She was breathing deeper and deeper, gulping for her breath.

"How about these people?" I asked. It was a photo of my mother and father reciting the Torah blessing. Fern didn't seem to have any idea who they were. "It's your brother Harry," I told her. "And my mom, Phyllis."

Now Fern's chest was heaving with increasing violence. "You have to get me out of here, Lee Richard," she said loudly. "They're going to kill me, Lee Richard. You need to take me away."

I put away the computer and wheeled her over to the desk.

"She's having a hallucination. I guess a bad one," I told the nurse. "I was showing her some photos. Maybe they upset her."

"It isn't the photos," the nurse said. "It's because the doctor won't let her smoke. We'll need to settle her down. It's probably best that you go."

I put my arm around Fern's shoulders, then said, "Take good care of her."

"We will." The nurse smiled. "We love Fern."

"So do I," I said. I leaned down and kissed Fern on the forehead. "Happy birthday," I whispered.

"Don't go, Lee Richard."

I squeezed her right shoulder and put my cheek on her head. "I'll be back soon," I promised. "Maybe in April, with the kids."

Later that afternoon, while I was waiting for the plane to Detroit, I checked my email and downloaded a recording of Loizzo's lecture from earlier in the week. It was called "Karma and Rebirth: Taking Responsibility for Self-Creation." Like many Westerners, I tended to use the word "karma" as a shorthand for "getting what you deserve"— as in, "One good or bad deed begets another." Or I used it to convey a sense of cosmic fate or luck—as in, "Jack tore his Achilles tendon again; that guy has the worst karma of anyone I know." I was interested in hearing Loizzo's definition of karma, and why he had linked karma to rebirth. Was he talking about reincarnation—the migration of the soul from one body to another? Or did he mean rebirth in the sense of being "born again"?

Once the plane leveled off at thirty thousand feet above sea level and the captain gave the go-ahead, I put on my headphones and began listening to Loizzo's lecture. It started, as usual, with a fifteen-minute mindfulness meditation, this time focusing on our sensations. Then he began to talk about how karma related to the Noble Truth of the Origin of Suffering. "Our suffering isn't caused by genetics, bad luck, or a curse from God," he said. "It's a result of our intentions and actions. It's a matter of cause and effect."

According to Loizzo, rebirth didn't involve the transmigration of a soul: It took place psychologically, as "a pattern of ego development across lifetimes, passed from one generation to the next." As part of their own ego development, children "imprint" many of their parents' habits and behaviors on their unconscious minds. If a child repeats a habit or behavior frequently enough, it becomes part of the child's character and nature.

I thought about my own childhood. From as far back as I could remember, my mother made a point of saying, "You can never trust other people." By "other people," she meant strangers who approached me on the street, my father's mother, and people who weren't Jewish. She reinforced this lesson in a variety of ways: by chastising me if I talked to a person she didn't know, by limiting my exposure to people who weren't Jewish, by telling me that the vast majority of people in the world cared "only about themselves," and by challenging me whenever I said anything positive about her mother-in-law, my Nana Shirley.

As I grew older, I realized that my mother inherited her distrust of other people from her own mother, my Nana Bertie, who was quick to find fault with anyone outside of her immediate family. Rejecting that parochial worldview, I tended to rush to the defense of the people my mother and grandmother savaged.

But here's the rub: Whenever I found myself criticizing other people at home or in the workplace, I'd deploy the same beady-eyed glare that my mother and grandmother used. I hated that suspicious, holier-than-thou look, yet it gradually became a predictable part of my own nature, to the point that Elizabeth could blunt a disparaging remark from me by saying, "Don't give me that beady-eyed look of yours."

When my mother and grandmother were angry at them, my father and grandfather would retreat into an impenetrable silence that infuriated their wives even more. I reacted to Elizabeth's fury the same way: by not acknowledging it. "That's all you're going to say to me? Nothing?" she'd say angrily at me. My mother used to say the same thing to my father.

These were merely two examples of how a pattern of behavior got passed from one generation of my family to the next, becoming part of my character and psychological makeup. But I wasn't condemned to repeat that pattern of behavior forever, according to Loizzo. "The Buddha said that we create our own happiness and our own suffering," he said. "We have the power to change."

But how?

"Buddha is as Buddha does," he said. It was a quote from his mentor Bob Thurman. It meant: If you do certain things, you become those things. If you're depressed and want to be happy, for instance, you need to gain a better understanding of what you do to depress yourself and stop doing those things. Then you need to figure out what makes you happy and begin doing those things. "Taking responsibility for self-creation is that simple," Loizzo said. "We can all do it."

Even me, I thought, as the flight attendant told us to turn off our various devices and store them under the seat. I made sure my seat belt was buckled. Then, as always, I gripped the arms of my seat in preparation for what turned out to be a relatively smooth and uneventful landing.

My hotel was modest and at the edge of a man-made lake in a Detroit suburb, maybe three miles from the leafy backyard where Rabbi Sherwin Wine had married Elizabeth and me fourteen years earlier under her father's favorite tree. After all the tragedies in Elizabeth's family, our wedding had ushered in an era of hope and happiness. But now, with Elizabeth's mother dead and my own parents living in Florida, Detroit held far less meaning for me. I'd be here two nights to give two talks, which would give me plenty of time to meditate—and to reflect on what I'd been learning.

After almost a year of spiritually shopping around, I still didn't have a regular meditation practice. Meditating at home had been nearly impossible because of the pets and noise. So I'd taken to meditating on the fly: for a few minutes at the end of a yoga class, or in the dog run when Pip and Mac were chasing their friends, or at the Dominican church on my way home from taking Noah to school. Those were usually the few times a day I could do it without a child or dog interrupting me.

I didn't have a set technique. Sometimes I'd focus on my breath, or try a loving-kindness meditation, or silently repeat the "Sohum" mantra. At the gym, while running on the treadmill, I might listen to one of Loizzo's guided mindfulness meditations, so that I could practice what he preached more effectively in my daily life. Instead of taking a middle-of-the-day nap to restore my energy, I'd lie on the floor or a mat for yoga nidra, a technique that uses focused breathing and moving awareness from one body part to another to induce a state of deep relaxation. Or I'd go outside for a walk. As the Zen Buddhist monk Thich Nhat Hanh taught, slow, conscious walking helps us calm down and appreciate our surroundings—and it can be done almost anywhere, energizing us.

As I tried to practice, or at least sample, these various forms of meditation, I also tried to educate myself in the growing number of scientific studies about the impact of meditation on the brain and well-being. In his research on long-term meditators, Andrew Newberg, a neuroscientist at the University of Pennsylvania, discovered that meditation increases activity in the front part of the brain (important to focused attention and decision making) while decreasing it in the parietal lobe, which orients us in space. That's why meditative states often involve major changes in spatial perception and a lost sense of self. A study at the University of California, Davis, showed that meditation increases telomerase activity in immune cells, contributing to a heightened sense of psychological well-being. Sara Lazar, a researcher at Massachusetts General Hospital, discovered that repeated practice of guided meditation can increase the density of gray matter in the hippocampus, which is crucial to learning and memory, and in structures associated with self-awareness, compassion, and introspection, while decreasing the density of gray matter in the amygdala, which plays an important role in anxiety and stress. A study of compassion-based meditation training at Emory University showed significant increases in neural activity in areas of the brain important for empathy, including the inferior frontal gyrus and dorsomedial prefrontal cortex.

I tried to keep in mind what both Loizzo and Salzberg said: There was no such thing as a perfect meditation; two minutes a day was better than none; and that you should experiment and not have any expectations.

I sat by the window in a straight-backed armchair—the kind you only seem to find in hotels. Outside, the late afternoon sun was going down. It was ridiculously quiet. No Mac, no Pip, no kids shouting across the room, no smell of dinner cooking, no voices from the street, no trucks rumbling by, no mindless TV chattering in the background.

Only my restless thoughts to distract me.

Most of them were about Fern. How imprisoned she seemed in

that disease, that body, that place. I imagined myself sitting in that tiny courtyard, strapped into that cold metallic wheelchair, looking up at the tiny patch of blue sky, those transient clouds, with absolutely nowhere to go. Unlike Fern, I had freedom. I had choices. I could choose to stay or go. To learn from my mistakes or keep repeating them. To make myself happy or sad.

I clicked on the MP3 and forwarded it to the meditation at the end of Loizzo's "Karma and Rebirth" lecture. He instructed us to become aware of the cool, fresh, nurturing air of the in-breath and to use the out-breath to expel the black smoke of everything toxic in our lives. I heard him say, "Let the gift of breath fill, smooth, and energize every cell of your body. Make this feeling of calm your home base, your place to recharge."

I opened my eyes. It was nearly seven o'clock. I had been meditating for twenty-seven minutes—a lot longer than usual—than ever, perhaps. Out the window of the hotel room I could see that the sun had set over the lake and the lights on the dock had come on. There were four of them, one at each corner, beacons in the gathering darkness—Buddha's Four Noble Truths, I mused.

Later that night I got a phone call from Caroline. She was sobbing hysterically.

"What's wrong?" I asked.

"It used to be fun being a twin," she said through her tears. "Now I hate it."

"Why?" I asked.

She listed three of the countless ways Ben made her suffer: "He ignores me. He says bad things about me. He wants my friends to like him more than they like me."

Clearly, Caroline was exaggerating. Ben had shown no special interest in her girlfriends. More likely one of them had flirted with him or laughed at his jokes, igniting Caroline's adolescent-girl insecurities.

I remembered something Loizzo had said: "We walk around with these open wounds that people keep bumping into. If you set your sights on righting every mean or wrong thing done to you, you'll have to become either a vigilante or a public defender."

Ben had bumped into one of Caroline's open wounds—and now she was trying to figure out how to retaliate.

"What Buddha said was, 'Heal the wound.' Correct your distorted perceptions of yourself. Once you do that, you can walk around and people can do mean and negative things to you and you'll feel fine," Loizzo had told us in class.

Caroline was clearly feeling too raw to benefit from that wisdom. So, instead, I reminded her that she'd been BFFs with the same three girls since kindergarten; that they loved and cherished her, as did her mom, dad, Noah, Pip, Mac, Sophie, and even Ben.

"Who, by far, is Grandpa Harry's favorite grandchild?" I asked.

"Caroline," she said softly.

"And who has absolutely the best laugh in the world?"

"Caroline," she said with a laugh.

"And who has the prettiest, smartest, funniest, and most generous daughter in the world?"

"You do, Daddy."

I could sense that Caroline had survived the storm; she was beginning to steady herself.

"Feeling better?"

"Definitely," she said.

"Sometimes we get all worked up and start seeing everything

and everyone in ways that have very little to do with the way things really are," I said on the phone. "We all do that. I do it. Mom does it. The President of the United States does it. We get all worked up and see things through a weirdly distorted lens. Including—especially—ourselves. I want you to remember one thing."

"What?" she said.

"When you feel angry, hopeless, and out of control, like you did today . . . when you're sure everyone's against you and you want to just shut the door and never come out again . . . when you want to kill someone—yourself even, and I mean that—remember that you're probably just seeing things through a fuzzy, distorted lens. Mom and I know what that's like, we really do, so we'll do every-thing we can to help you see things more clearly, to help you feel better about yourself, to help you learn to keep yourself from feeling so crazy and out of control again. Okay?"

There was a long pause as she wiped away the last of her tears.

"Okay," she said before hanging up. "Thanks, Daddy. I love you, Daddy."

I had drawn heavily upon the wisdom of Buddha and Bodhisattva Joe in that conversation. And it seemed to work. While looking for God, I was beginning to develop better parenting skills. Ten years earlier, when the planes struck and Ben was terrified that the terror-ists would kill him and us, I wasn't sure I'd ever have the words and wisdom I'd need to guide my kids through the challenges they'd face growing up. My own parents had reacted way too often out of fear and superstition, as had their parents and grandparents before them. I had inherited those inclinations. But my conversation that afternoon with my daughter had felt like a breakthrough for me, or at the very least one small step in stopping the cycle of reactiveness

and recrimination that had brought so much suffering to generations of my family.

The topic of the class after Thanksgiving was the Buddha's Third
Noble Truth—the Truth of the Cessation of Suffering. Many ex-
perts called it the most important of the four truths, since it posited
the concept of Nirvana.

Loizzo began by correcting what he called the "biggest miscon-
ception" Westerners have about Nirvana: "We've grown up in a
culture that describes heaven as a magical place like the Land of Oz.
So we tend to think of Nirvana that way."

I never believed in heaven when I was a kid, but I did have a
picture of how it worked: First you die; then your soul leaves your
body; then it goes straight to that shimmering blue place in the
sky—a place like Oz. At least, that's how my Catholic friends explained it to me: While the souls of non-Christians like me went to
hell, the souls of Christians went to Oz.

That's not true, Loizzo said. "Nirvana is not a place. It's simply
the end of something."

Buddhists likened Nirvana to blowing out a candle. When we
blow out the red-hot flame of our habitual suffering, it leaves a trail
of smoke, then nothing at all.

Did you need to die in order to experience Nirvana?

Not at all, Loizzo said. "Anytime you go into a meditative state
and slow your mind down, you experience a temporary cessation of
your afflictions," he explained. "Because your mind is no longer
intent on getting what it craves, the connection between 'I'll get
this' and 'I'll be happy' gets broken. In the process, you realize that

you've been seeking happiness in the wrong places . . . that you can be blissfully happy . . . if only you'd see things as they are."

So you could get a taste of Nirvana by meditating and experiencing what it feels like to stop suffering for a few minutes. Nirvana, as Loizzo explained it, was "the cumulative result of many—if not infinite—smaller cessations."

I couldn't tell whether he was talking about Buddha's Nirvana or his own idiosyncratic take on it. (I suspected the latter.) But I did see where he was headed. Those small cessations could happen anywhere: during breakfast, in a clothing store, stuck in traffic on the way to work. Whenever you felt threatened or craved something bad for yourself, you had a chance to add one more notch to your Nirvana belt. Got anger? Got frustration? Got an uncontrollable need for another drink? Loizzo's prescription for easing your emotional pain was simple: "Stop. Take three deep breaths. And ask yourself: *What am I feeling?*"

When you did that, a space would open up between you and your behavior. In that space, you could see what was bugging you more clearly and respond to it more skillfully. As the smaller cessations added up, you'd find yourself building a reservoir of peace and clarity that would help you fight your future demons. Then one day, when you least expected it, the flame of your suffering would blow out: Nirvana!

Loizzo said that there was another way to look at it: through the Fourth Noble Truth, which outlines Buddha's Eightfold Path to the Cessation of Suffering. The Eightfold Path consists of Right View, Right Intention, Right Speech, Right Action, Right Livelihood, Right Effort, Right Mindfulness, and Right Concentration. Because of its connotation of "the One and Only," Loizzo said he preferred the words "Perfect," "Realistic," "Appropriate," and even

"Groovy," to "Right." He liked the word "Skillful"—as in Skillful Speech, Action, and Effort—best of all. But you could also see the Eightfold Path as a living commitment to such positive values as being helpful, telling the truth, reconciling differences, being generous, bringing people together, working for peace—the same values at the heart of Quakerism.

As he had done earlier in the course, Loizzo urged us to follow Buddha's Eightfold Path step-by-step, like a cookbook. He compared it to the way the 12 steps in the modern recovery movement work. Both Buddha and 12-step focus on reversing the attitudes and behaviors that feed addiction. For example, Step 4 calls on recovering addicts to "make a fearless searching inventory" of themselves—and to share that inventory with "another person or God." That sort of shared honesty is at the heart of the Buddhist principle of Right Speech. Step 9 calls for addicts to make amends to the people they have harmed. "It means cleaning house with the world—and putting our relationships on a clean, sober, fair footing," Loizzo said. This is the spirit underlying the principle of Right Livelihood in Buddhism.

The goal in both Buddhism and 12-step programs is inner peace. "You can't plant a violence seed and get a peace tree," he said. "To get a peace tree, you need to plant a peace seed."

Perhaps that's what I had been doing by pursuing so many pathways to God: planting peace seeds, with the hope that one of them would grow into a tree, offering shade and sustenance for my soul.

In the last class, Loizzo told us his theory of why people signed up for courses like "Self-Healing and the Contemplative Life."

"We want to go to our relatives' house and not get stressed out," he said.

I definitely got what he was saying.

When I was young, I loved our family get-togethers, particularly the ones that took place at my grandparents' house. After I left for college, though, I began to dread them, because those few hours in my relatives' presence would erase all the progress I had made toward becoming an adult. Because the dashed hopes and lingering expectations of my childhood would surface again. Because, no matter how much I tried not to care, my ears would turn into hypersensitive antennae alert to a lifetime of slights and disappointments. Because a voice from deep down inside me would cry out: *Why can't you just love me for who I am?*

All that hurt around the table—the decades of broken promises, distorted perceptions, and mythic wrongs—had been passed down through generations of my family like a toxic heirloom. It stressed me out.

So I got why people like me would sign up for a class that promised to help them heal and move on in their lives. The other reason I signed up for his class was that, reading Karen Armstrong and Huston Smith, I had become uncomfortable with Buddha's decision to abandon his family before seeking enlightenment. It reminded me of what Jesus had said: that you couldn't be a true disciple unless you hated your family and rejected everything about your life.

If I had followed Buddha's example or done as Jesus demanded, I would have had to give up either my family or my spiritual life. At least, that's what I thought before Loizzo's class. Now, after seeing the Buddha through Loizzo's eyes, I had a different view: It wasn't your family you needed to abandon; it was your toxic family heirloom, with its residue of cravings and addictions. Then you could "go forth," as Buddha had, on your search for enlightenment while remaining an everyday member of your family.

But the path to Nirvana is strewn with obstacles, as Loizzo was quick to point out. Go it alone, and you're vulnerable to giving up, falling short, losing steam. "It took one village to make you a neurotic," Loizzo said. "It will take another village to heal you." That's why Nirvana seekers need what Buddha called the "Three Reliances": a buddha, a dharma, and a sangha.

A buddha is a teacher, friend, or contemplative person who makes you feel that your goal is achievable. A dharma is a set of reproducible principles and practices that provides you with a step-by-step cookbook for achieving your goal. A sangha is a community of fellow seekers who cheer each other on, particularly when the spiritual going gets tough.

Looking back at my own journey thus far:

The Quakers had provided me with a dharma (as set forth in the pamphlet *Faith and Practice*) and potentially a sangha (the Morningside Meeting). But they didn't offer me a teacher who could help me integrate the dharma into my everyday life.

Loizzo had been a buddha, of sorts. He had tailored Buddha's dharma—the Four Noble Truths—to the spiritual needs of our modern Western society. His idiosyncratic blend of ancient Mahayana, modern psychology, and brain science had given me many useful insights, for which I was grateful, but I sensed that he would be only one of many such spiritual teachers for me and that, ultimately, I'd need a teacher with whom I'd have more give-and-take.

My fellow seekers at Tibet House were not a sangha for me: We simply shared the same space during Loizzo's lectures. So, contrary to what Loizzo had said and hoped, I never saw myself as a bubble floating in a sea of bubbles; I had continued floating alone.

It had been almost a year since I had stumbled onto the Belief-O-Matic quiz after my night of frightening chest pains. The quiz had armed me with a list of religions that might match my beliefs and the notion that I might shop around in various spiritual traditions, but without a way to start. As I had been contemplating a way to begin, Katherine had knocked on my door and kicked off the first leg of my journey—into the Quaker world of silent worship. Eight months later, my wife gave me a statue of Buddha, which became my muse as I embarked on the second leg of my journey—into Buddhism as seen through the eyes of a Harvard-educated shrink who had shaped a dharma for self-healing from the Four Noble Truths and the latest research on the plasticity of the human brain.

Now I was ready to start down a new path in my shopping expedition for God. What would it be? And who would point the way?

Silent Night, Holy Night

December

It was December 23, around noon, and I was about to Skype my parents so that I could wish them a happy anniversary. My cell phone started vibrating. It was my Uncle Pudge, calling from Denver. The connection was bad, and I walked to the window, where the reception would be better. Outside, on the street, I could see the darkened shapes of my neighbors pushing home against the snow.

"Hear me now?" Pudge asked.

"Yes," I said. "You're coming in better."

"Fernie's dead. I just got a call from her social worker. She died last night in the hospital—heart attack."

I didn't know what to say, so I kept looking out the window. A gust off the river blew the snow east, toward the corner of 110th Street and Broadway. There, in front of the Rite Aid drugstore, the last two rows of Christmas trees were being sold by the long-haired nomads who had come down from Montreal the day after Thanksgiving. Today was Thursday. By Sunday, the day after Christmas, they'd be gone.

"Fern dead?" I finally said. I couldn't believe it. Six weeks earlier I had listened to her talk about her nightmares and showed her pictures of the twins' b'nai mitzvah and promised to visit her again. I knew her health was deteriorating but I had never really considered the possibility that I'd never see her again.

My aunt had been so afraid of dying alone. "Was anyone there to hold her hand?" I wanted to ask. But that wasn't the type of thing Pudge would have known.

"You coming?" he asked.

"I can't," I said. "Because of the blizzard, the airports here are closed."

Pudge called me back a few hours later to discuss the details of the funeral. I was glad that Fern would be getting her wish: She'd be buried next to my Uncle Jerry. I only hoped that someone besides Pudge and the rabbi would be there to say Kaddish.

The next day, I wasn't in the mood for anything festive, not even Katherine's annual Christmas Eve party. "Do I really have to go?" I asked Elizabeth. I couldn't imagine making small talk with gourmands and oenophiles while my thoughts were hundreds of miles away in Cleveland.

"Of course you do," Elizabeth said. "Katherine is one of our best friends in the world. You—we—have to go."

At 8:00 P.M., we left our apartment and took the elevator up to Katherine's. I tried my best to look like I was enjoying myself. I smiled politely as I sipped champagne and exchanged holiday greetings. But the fact was, I wanted to be in Cleveland with Pudge, remembering Fern, or alone in a dark room. I didn't want to squander the significance of the moment.

At a little after 9:00 P.M., our neighbor Jackie asked if anyone at the party was interested in going to Christmas Eve Mass with her: She had an extra ticket. When no one stepped forward, I looked over at Elizabeth. She nodded, her sign that I had done my duty and was free to go. Jackie waited for me in the lobby while I got my coat and gloves. Then we stepped out into the bone-chilling cold. All down the street, doormen were shoveling the sidewalks in front of their buildings and teens were tossing snowballs at passing cars. We forged ahead. As we turned the corner at the next block, we could see dark shapes scurrying up the stairs of the cathedral and through its huge bronze doors.

Against the wintry sky, the cathedral looked like a hulking gray ship. From "bow" to "stern," the Cathedral of Saint John the Divine is 601 feet long. At 11,200 square feet, it is the fourth-largest church building in the world. It is also famous for its Great Organ, its progressive politics, and its annual celebrations of Christmas, New Year's, Easter, and the winter solstice, featuring some of the world's best-known musicians.

By the time we took our seats, nearly two thousand people had gathered in the cavernous cathedral to sing hymns and celebrate what the bishop called "the greatest gift ever given"—the birth of Jesus. Looking around, I felt a moment of what-in-the-world-is-a-Jewish-boy-like-me-doing-in-a-place-like-this guilt. But then I found myself swept away by the sound of the organ playing a medley of "The First Noel," "O Little Town of Bethlehem," and "Angels We Have Heard on High." Soon I was singing softly: "It came upon the midnight clear . . ." And then I was singing with all my heart: "Peace on earth, good will to men, from heaven's all-gracious King."

After months of listening for God deep inside myself and in the stories I heard at Quaker meetings, after weeks of practicing mindfulness under the guidance of an agnostic Buddhist psychiatrist, after a day wrestling with the meaning of my aunt's life and death, I had joined a gathering of my neighbors to praise God and pray for peace. Now a deep hum was rising from my diaphragm, pulsating in my chest, vibrating in my throat, and bursting into cathartic, communal song.

So much of my journey to this point had been a silent one, with eyes closed, looking for the Divine within. It had focused on being disciplined, attentive to my own breath, so that I could see my thoughts and emotions for what they really were—the stuff of passing clouds.

So much of my journey had been a still one, with legs crossed, palms folded, hands in a gesture of witness and understanding.

So much of my journey had been about learning to listen. To people who had suffered loss, heartbreak, self-doubt, and fears of dying.

Now it seemed to be taking a different turn, toward one filled with song. Standing shoulder to shoulder with my neighbor Jackie and thousands of strangers, I was singing the praises of God.

Singing out would add a new dimension to my search for God—of that I was certain. But would Christianity provide the score? As much as I enjoyed singing Christmas carols and hearing the Nativity story, I couldn't get excited about the theology of it all, especially the Nicene Creed, with its droning statement of belief in an abstract Trinity and "in One, Holy, Catholic and Apostolic Church." Nor could I embrace the idea that the Holy Spirit had transubstantiated the wafer and wine of Communion into the flesh and blood of the child whose birthday we were celebrating.

And yet, as this Christmas Eve Mass came to an end, I was feeling the same deep yearning that had led me to go on my God walks, accompany Katherine to Quaker meetings, learn meditation from Sharon Salzberg, study Buddhism with Joe Loizzo, and trudge through the snow to the Cathedral of Saint John the Divine earlier that evening, seeking solace in song.

The ushers went row to row passing out little battery-operated candles. When we each had one, the bishop instructed us to flick them on, and two thousand candles suddenly illuminated the cathedral, marking Christ's birth and mankind's passage through the long, dark night of one more winter.

"Silent night, holy night, all is calm, all is bright."

For the past hour we had been singing our hearts out in praise of God. And now God was restoring our hope, easing our pain, bringing us together. In Joe Loizzo's class, I had struggled mightily to imagine myself a bubble in a sea of bubbles. But here, with my candle in hand and my voice vibrating in a great chorus of voices, I could see "that which is God in everyone" in two thousand glowing faces.

"May you live in safety, be happy, be healthy, live with ease." I said this quietly, to myself, for every sentient being in the cathedral and on earth.

"Joy to the world!" I sang out triumphantly, and kept humming as I walked out the huge bronze doors into the chill Manhattan night.

part three

Season of Song and Praise

Divine sound is the cause of all manifestation. The knower of the mystery of sound knows the mystery of the whole universe.

—Hazrat Inayat Khan

Good Vibrations

January Through September

That winter, as one of our New Year's resolutions, Elizabeth and I began taking a weekly hot yoga class at a nearby studio. For seventy-five minutes, in 105-degree heat, we'd move through a sequence of twenty-six asanas that stretched every muscle and tendon in our bodies, giving us, as the teacher said, "the most thorough and detoxifying workout known to man."

Neither of us had any spiritual expectations of the class; we saw it as a chance to work out together, as we had enjoyed doing before the twins were born and parenting took over, and to lose a few pounds. During the first few sessions, I was mainly aware of how much we sweated—the heat was beastly, intolerable, yet we pushed through. Then, in the fourth class, I noticed a feeling of being transported to a deeply emotional place. It wasn't the heat or the postures that took me there; it was the music. The teacher played a mix-tape of New Age music during class, most of which didn't do anything for me—it was ambient, ethereal, meant to relax you or move you along.

There was one song, however, that made me want to simultaneously cry and shout for joy. Its singer chanted, "Om Namah Shivaya," over and over again in a low baritone that rumbled like distant thunder. The song started out slowly, contemplatively. Then it picked up steam, with the singer pausing so that we, the listeners, could respond to what he'd just chanted by repeating the same phrase. I had no idea what the words meant, but they seemed to hang in the air like a blessing or incantation that invoked a higher being.

The teacher told me that the chanter's name was Krishna Das and that "Namah Shivaya" was the first track on his 1998 CD *Pilgrim Heart*. I bought the CD that same night, as much for its title as for the music. I couldn't think of a better way to describe my own heart's longing for God.

Previously, only two other artists had put me so consistently in the mood for contemplation and prayer: jazz pianist Keith Jarrett and tenor saxophonist John Coltrane. I must have listened to the recording of Jarrett's 1975 concert in Köln, Germany, a thousand times since I first heard it in college, mainly on rainy afternoons. The shouts and whispers of Jarrett's playing, his sharp pauses and pondering turns, would wake up my slumbering spirit with the promise of a new day. Coltrane's *A Love Supreme* was my go-to music when I felt emotionally shattered: I could count on the blend of his soaring saxophone and Elvin Jones's earthbound drumming to put the pieces of my eggshell self back together again and fill me with gratitude for being alive.

Krishna Das's chanting could be just as transcendent as the music of these artists, but it was also more confessional, intimate, and communal. You didn't just listen to "Namah Shivaya," you chanted along, becoming part of its creation, adding your voice and your longings to those of spiritual seekers throughout the world.

The mantras, repeated over and over again, were as easy to remember as nursery rhymes: "Raadhe Raadhe, Govinda Govinda / Raadhe Raadhe, Govinda Govinda / Govinda Bhaja Govinda / Govinda Bhaja Govinda." I didn't yet know what those Sanskrit words meant or signified. But I found myself singing them anyway. Louder and louder. Faster and faster. The vibrations moved from my belly to my chest, from my chest to my throat, from my throat to my lips, into the vibrational field of wherever I happened to be standing.

Perhaps the most revealing moment on *Pilgrim Heart* comes five minutes into a song called "Mountain Hare Krishna," when all the Hares give way to that most familiar of Christian hymns: "Amazing Grace." In his rumbling baritone Krishna Das sings, "Amazing grace! How sweet the sound / That sav'd a soul, a soul like me! / I once was lost, but now I'm found / Was blind, so blind, but now I see." You sense that the pilgrim—Krishna Das—has led a profligate life, he's stumbled into a dark alley, blinded by his ambitions and addictions. Right when he's about to give up all hope: "Amazing grace!" The sweet sound of his own chanting saves him from his life of wretched, directionless wandering.

Was I right? Did chanting save Krishna Das from despair? And why did I feel so drawn to this man and his music?

He was born Jeffrey Kagel in New York City in 1947. His family was Jewish. Growing up on Long Island, he dreamed of becoming a blues singer. He attended college at the State University of New York in Stony Brook and then New Paltz, where he got turned on to Asian culture and religion, just as Sharon Salzberg had at around the same time.

When he was twenty-one, Kagel met Ram Dass (formerly Richard Alpert), a spiritual teacher who had been Timothy Leary's research partner in the Harvard Psilocybin Project that helped launch the psychedelic movement of the 1960s. Ram Dass had just returned from India, where he had become a devotee of Neem Karoli Baba, the Hindu guru known as Maharaj-ji.

In 1970, Kagel followed his friend's example and traveled to India. The rest is history. Maharaj-ji put him on the path of chanting, and Kagel changed his name to Krishna Das, which in Sanskrit means "servant to Krishna," the Hindu god of love. It took twenty years of chanting and praying and figuring things out before Krishna Das felt comfortable enough to chant in public. But when he finally did, in the mid-1990s, he found an eager audience. By the time I heard a recording of him in yoga class, he was perhaps the most famous devotional chanter in the world.

I wanted to know why Krishna Das's music spoke so deeply to me. And, more broadly, why music had been a core activity of our species' spiritual life since the Paleolithic era. I read that researchers at McGill University had recently demonstrated music's biochemical appeal. When we listen to "peak emotional moments in music"— for example, the first four notes in Beethoven's Fifth Symphony— the neurotransmitter dopamine is released in the striatum, an ancient part of the human brain that responds to the pleasure created by such triggers as food, sex, and cocaine. In other words, the part of our brain that enables us to remember, imagine, and create music—the auditory cortex—is tied to our body's ancient motivational and reward system. Knowing this, it made sense that hearing Krishna Das sing "Mountain Hare Krishna," with its seamless shift into "Amazing Grace," affected me so deeply—the song was making an impression on me at a cellular level, leading me to want to hear it again.

Besides my biochemical response to the music, I was also aesthetically moved by the phrasing and tonality of the Sanskrit words. Like many of the world's religions, Hinduism invests a great deal of power in a handful of words and sounds. In fact, both Hinduism and the great Abrahamic religions (Judaism, Islam, and Christianity) believe that the world came into being ex nihilo (out of nothing) through a sacred word or vibrational sound. Vedic scripture, the basis of Hindu thought, says that the universe was created "by divine utterance." In the Bible, "God said, 'Let there be Light / And there was Light." John 1:1 refined the theme: "In the Beginning was the Word, and the Word was with God, and the Word was God."

God's word had the power to create an entire universe, and the sacred name of God had the power to change a person's life, according to the early Christians. The most important prayer in Christianity goes: "Our Father, who art in heaven, hallowed be thy name." And if you say God's sacred name with the proper intent and devotion, the payoff can be quite consequential. As the Apostle Paul said: "Whoever calls upon the Lord's name shall be saved."

As for repetition: The more you pray to God, the closer you get to God, according to most religions. In Eastern Orthodoxy, for instance, the preferred "mantra" for repetitive prayer is, "Lord Jesus, son of God, have mercy on me, a sinner." I once met a Greek Orthodox monk who said without any hint of boasting that he repeats "The Jesus Prayer" day and night, as he works, reads, and even sleeps. That's about as close as a person can get to fulfilling the commandment, "Pray, ceaselessly!" (1 Thessalonians 5:17). By saying the name of the Divine—in an attitude of humility and devotion— many religions say that you become more present to and intimate with the Divine.

The notion of praying ceaselessly is inconceivable for most of us.

I know some pretty good multitaskers, but it's hard to imagine any of them developing a facility to pray constantly as they cook, talk on the phone, make deals, help their children with homework, catch a baseball, pay a bill, or do even one of the multitude of everyday tasks that consumes their energy and brainpower at any given moment. Praying, to most people, is an occasional or ritualistic activity done at prescribed times of the day (for example, at bedtime or before a meal); in the context of a religious service or observance; or when appealing for Divine guidance, intervention, or aid, as athletes do before a game and so many of us do when a loved one is ill.

Because I was incapable of doing even two things effectively at the same time, it was unlikely that I'd achieve a deeper connection with the Divine through ceaseless, or even frequent, prayer. But maybe a more ecstatic type of prayer would do the trick.

The ecstatic chanting of God's name is part of numerous religious traditions. Psalm 150, 4–5 goes: "Glory ye in his holy name. Praise him with timbrel and dance. Praise him with stringed instruments and organs. Praise him upon the loud cymbals. Praise him upon the high-sounding cymbals." Ascribed to King David, the psalm evokes an image of the ancient Hebrews dancing in front of the First and Second Temples. But to worshippers of other traditions it could just as easily bring to mind Sufis whirling or Baptists calling out, "Glory, glory, hallelujah!" in God's name.

God and God's name are one and the same in Hinduism. As a result, chanting God's names can help unite the chanter physically and spiritually with God: a notion at the roots of kirtan (pronounced keer-ton), the call-and-response Congregational form of singing practiced by Krishna Das.

*　　　*　　　*

In late August, Krishna Das was scheduled to perform along with other devotional chanters at Omega, a holistic wellness and education center only a few minutes from my home in upstate New York. I asked Elizabeth if she wanted to accompany me, since she was also a fan of Krishna Das's music. When she snapped, "No," I wasn't surprised.

My wife loves all kinds of music, particularly Broadway show tunes, but she has always had a terrible voice. In seventh grade, no one wanted to stand next to her in music class. Her relatives (including her children) made fun of her whenever she opened her mouth to sing. Whenever she chanted, "Om," in yoga class, people strained to see which of their fellow students was responsible for the donkey-like braying that threw the whole class woefully off-key. The sad irony of Elizabeth's life was that the human activity that gave her the most pleasure—music—also gave her the deepest pain. It would have been hard for her to endure, much less enjoy, an entire weekend of chanting.

Before I headed upstate to Omega, I spent several days reading about the historical roots of Hindu devotional chanting. Kirtan originated in sixth century India, with Hindu singer/poets who would roam the countryside emphasizing the heart instead of ritual in their songs. In the sixteenth century, it became associated with Sri Chaitanya Mahaprabhu, a proponent of the Vaishnava school of Bhakti (devotional) yoga, who lived from 1486 to 1534 in the Bengal region of northern India.

Sri Chaitanya is often compared to three of history's other great spiritual innovators. Like Buddha, he was a family man who became a monk. Like Saint Francis of Assisi, he loved nature and was allegedly able to soothe savage beasts with his songs. Like Jesus, he was said to have cured lepers and fed the masses—not with bread but with mangoes.

At a time when holy men stressed strict study of Vedic scripture and long hours of meditation, Sri Chaitanya wandered the streets of his native Bengal chanting and dancing in blissful devotion to Lord Krishna. In fact, his followers, known as Gaudiya Vaishnavas, considered Sri Chaitanya to be the full incarnation of Krishna, which is how he's viewed today by the International Society of Krishna Consciousness, better known as the Hare Krishna movement. If you've ever seen a group of Hare Krishnas singing and dancing in public in their bright saffron robes, with their shaved heads, shaking cymbals, and beating on double-headed drums, you've experienced part of Sri Chaitanya's legacy.

Sri Chaitanya left eight verses of instructions for his followers. In one verse, he wrote that chanting the holy names of the Lord "cleanses the heart" and "extinguishes the fire of conditional life, of repeated birth and death." In another, he wrote that the Lord has "hundreds of millions of names" and it is through these names—for example, Krishna and Govinda—that devotees can "easily approach" the Lord. In another, he wrote that a devotee should chant the holy names in "a humble state of mind, thinking oneself lower than the straw in the street."

He claimed that he didn't want wealth, women, or fame: "O almighty Lord . . . I only want Your causeless devotional service birth after birth." That meant chanting the Lord's name until it consumed him. "Oh my Lord," he wrote, "when will my eyes be decorated with tears of love flowing constantly when I chant Your holy name? When will my voice choke up, and when will the hairs of my body stand on end at the recitation of Your name?"

Shakespeare may have written, "What's in a name? That which we call a rose / By any other name would smell as sweet." But Sri Chaitanya, like many of history's leading spiritual figures, believed that the holy names of God were all-important, all-powerful, and the closest we humans could come to having an experience of the Divine. By repeating the names of God over and over again in an attitude of pure devotion, we could be transported into a deep spiritual state and achieve union with the deity. I wondered, would that happen to me?

On Friday night, before the first chanting session, I had dinner in Omega's huge communal dining hall across from two middle-aged women from McLean, Virginia. Debbie, a chatty and upbeat brunette, had attended the previous year's ecstatic chant weekend. Now she wanted to share the experience with her friend Elaine, whom she'd met at a Buddhist meditation retreat. I wondered what Buddhists like them were doing at a gathering of Hindu devotional singers. "We're meaning junkies," Elaine said with a laugh.

When we entered the lecture hall on the Omega campus, we encountered a few hundred other meaning junkies waiting for the chanting to begin. For the most part, they seemed indistinguishable from the ones who had attended the classes I had taken at Tibet House. As usual, there were far more women than men in the crowd. Most were sitting on meditation cushions or folded-up blankets. Several young women were doing dance stretches and yoga postures in the back of the hall. Just about everyone, including me, was wearing some type of yoga attire.

Over the next few hours we'd get a taste of what lay ahead for the weekend. Jai Uttal (born Douglas Zion Uttal, in Brooklyn, New York, in 1951) kicked off the evening with a kirtan called "Jai Jai Ma!" (Jai, as in his name, means "victory" in Hindi, and "Jai Jai Ma," as in the chant, means "Victory to the Divine Feminine.")

Strumming his guitar to a reggae beat, he'd repeat the phrase over and over again, in various iterations, accompanied by a flutist and tabla player. And we'd chant each phrase after him.

Like Ram Dass and Krishna Das, Jai Uttal is a devotee of Neem Karoli Baba. He is also a Grammy Award–winning musician. He earned his chops in the early 1970s, wandering around the Bengal region of India with the Bauls, a sect of minstrels who seek unity with God through song. During the past twenty years, Jai Uttal became best known for his fusion of Hindu devotional chanting with jazz, blues, reggae, ska, and samba. But his music has always been grounded in japa—the repetition of God's names. He urged us to "enjoy God" while we chanted over the next three days. "By singing these prayers we join a stream of consciousness and devotion that has been flowing for centuries," he said. "You'll find yourself howling, growling, beseeching, and just when you think you've had enough, the blessings will pour down on you."

Next came kirtan's "first couple"—Deva Premal and Miten. In the 1960s, Miten (née Andy Desmond) had been a promising British rock-and-roller. Then he traveled to Pune, India, and became a devotee of Rajneesh, the controversial Hindu holy man known later as Osho. At Rajneesh's Pune ashram, Miten fell in love with Deva, an angelic young German with long blond hair and a celestial voice. Since 1990, they have been traveling the world singing kirtan together. They were so charming and comfortable with each other, so obviously in love, so harmonious in their singing, that they seemed like the living embodiment of Hinduism's most dynamic couple: Krishna and Radha.

By now, dozens of young and middle-aged women, and several men, too, were twirling dervishlike in the back of the hall, their arms raised to the sky. C. C. White, the "Aretha Franklin of Kirtan," as she is known, was in the house—and she was wearing a billowy red dress, a red head wrap, and huge circular earrings. She ended her set by chanting in English: "As we leave this place / Touched by Grace / Spread some love over and over again." Chanting along, I noticed how my breathing had become deeper and easier over the course of the night, and that I had achieved a state of feeling restfully alert, a combination of clearheaded and calm, as I did during my most satisfying meditation sessions. Yes, I felt touched by grace and full of love for God and my fellow meaning junkies in the room.

I didn't call Elizabeth that first night, but I did think of how much she would have disliked being there, in a place where God's name was so continually invoked, chanted, and praised. It emphasized the distance between us: We weren't even close, on the spiritual level, to being Miten and Deva, which both saddened me and frightened me. At the beginning of our marriage, there had been such a deep sense of mutual discovery in almost everything we did. Our newborn twins depended on us for everything, and pushing through our exhaustion, we were rewarded with the joy of first words, first steps, and first days of school. Like billions of couples before us, we set out on the essential human adventures of making babies, building a home, and raising children together. But during this newest chapter of our lives, I felt like I was going on a solo journey, which would involve ecstatic and intimate experiences with people who were not my wife and children. The tug-of-war between the life I had and the faith I was seeking was beginning to unnerve me.

As I chanted along with the kirtan wallahs, I was beginning to appreciate how carefully constructed the Sanskrit mantras had been to serve as "spiritual tools." The rishis (or sages) who wrote the mantras had a particularly resonant language to work with. According to Russill Paul, the kirtan singer and scholar, Sanskrit was developed systematically to include the natural progressions of sounds as created in the human mouth. The rich phonetics of Sanskrit strike the palate at multiple reflex points. As a result, writes Paul, certain mantras stimulate energy in "numerous meridians that awaken dormant parts of the brain," enhancing the circulation and flow of energy throughout the body.

The most sacred (and well-known) phrase in Sanskrit is "Om." That particular spelling leads Midwesterners like Elizabeth and me to pronounce it like we do "O-hio" or "O-klahoma," which is wrong. The spelling "A-u-m" reflects the mantra's deeper meaning: *A* is the first vowel in Sanskrit; *U* is the last. *M* is the final consonant. It took me a while to learn how to pronounce "Om" like "A-u-m," but when I did, I realized how it should be said in a way that enables you to approach the word with respect, taking time to articulate the first two vowel sounds.

"In the Beginning was the Word," Christians say. Hindus say, "In the Beginning was the sound of Om." The earliest Vedic texts, including the Upanishads and *Rig Veda*, begin with the word. In other spiritual traditions, we find the sound of Om all over the place: in the Hebrew word "shalom" (peace); the Hebrew affirmation "amen"; the Latin prefix "omni" (all or every); and in the English words that describe God as being omnipresent, omnipotent, and omniscient. It is difficult, when you see the interrootedness of so many religious traditions, to conclude that any one religion has an exclusive claim to the spiritual Truth.

*   *   *

Finally it was time for Krishna Das to begin. I had been waiting for this moment, as had the rest of the people who had signed up for the weekend. There was something so, well, American and professorial about Krishna Das as he walked toward the stage. He had a short gray beard and hair, wore wire-rimmed glasses, his red-and-black-plaid shirt was open to the waist over a bright red T-shirt. His outfit was deceptive, however, because red is, in fact, the color of his favorite Hindu god: Hanuman, the apelike humanoid who stars in the *Ramayana*, the Indian epic that tells the story of Rama's war against the demon king Ravana. Indeed, Krishna Das's first chant of the evening was his famously playful version of the "Hanuman Chalisa," which traditionally consists of forty verses detailing Hanuman's courage and strength, and his devotion to Rama, the Lord of Virtue and Self-Control.

Throughout a set that included many of his best-known songs, Krishna Das urged us to be patient with ourselves, the universe, and God. In perhaps his most moving chant, he kept referring to his "foolish heart," which doesn't seem to ever learn, once and for all, that there is "nowhere else to turn" except to God. He based the song on "Bhaja Govindam," an eighth century hymn by the great saint Adi Shankaracharya. "If we know anything about a path at all, it's only because of the great ones that have gone before us," Krishna Das said. "Out of their love and kindness, they have left some footprints for us to follow. So, in the same way that they wish for us, we wish that all beings everywhere, including ourselves, be safe, be happy, have good health, and enough to eat. And may we all live at ease of heart with whatever comes to us in life." When he said these heartfelt words, my thoughts flew to Elizabeth. May she sing with more ease, so that she can feel truly happy. And be much more likely to say yes the next time I ask her to accompany me for a weekend of ecstatic chanting.

*   *   *

There seems to be a common generational story behind many of these prominent kirtan wallahs. Like me, they were born in the 1950s and came from secular Jewish families that had only a tenuous, nostalgic connection to the religion of their forefathers. As teenagers they took drugs, had their egos shattered, and went off to India in search of adventure and enlightenment. They found themselves at the feet of a guru like Maharaj-ji or Rajneesh, who broke them even further, then built them back up and made them whole. By giving them an unconditional love they had never imagined, their guru earned their unquestioning devotion. Eventually the gurus sent these lost-and-found Westerners back home, assigning them the mission of enlightening the spiritually adrift West with meditation, prana, yoga, Vedas, and the stories of the various colorful gods, or devas, who represent the many forms of Brahman, the supreme Hindu god. Off they went, singing kirtan, playing tabla, teaching yoga postures, blowing minds, and opening hearts—all in and through the holy names of the Lord.

To all these kirtan wallahs—Jai Uttal, Krishna Das, the others—their guru was everything. In his impassioned autobiography, *Chants of a Lifetime*, Krishna Das wrote of Maharaj-ji: "For me, he's like the sun, just shining on everyone and everything. . . . He never required us to be something other than what we were . . . he loved us in spite of ourselves. He wanted us to accept ourselves for what we are, with all our shortcomings."

Maharaj-ji died in 1973. "I couldn't take life in his absence," wrote Krishna Das. He avoided chanting, which deepened his sense of loss. "Because when Maharaj-ji died, I thought I had lost my only chance to ever be happy, because being with him physically was the only thing that ever worked for me. So when he wasn't there, what could I do? I was helpless."

While Wah! (pronounced WAAH) was chanting, I took a seat in the back of the hall, a row behind where Krishna Das sat listening to her. He was trying his best to be alone and invisible. I sensed how hard he must work to chant for the right reasons—for his guru and not his ego, out of love and not pride.

Wah! (her legal name is Wah Deva; she's a graduate of the Oberlin Conservatory of Music) struggled to achieve that same balance and authenticity in her singing.

"I can't teach you how to chant," she told the audience. "You just do it and see what happens. It's the intention of your heart that matters, not the words, not the melody. Put your hand on your hearts and say Om. You'll feel your bones vibrating. I consider every note a deity."

Although Wah! had a different guru—hers was Amma, who is famed for hugging her followers—their relationship reminded me of the one Krishna Das had with Maharaj-ji. In one of her songs, she characterized herself as "a child of unwedded love." She sang, "I'm in so much trouble / Amma can you save me / Can you free the burden of my heart."

Like Krishna Das, she portrayed herself as a wounded child, in need of her guru's unconditional love. I couldn't really identify with that sentiment. As deficient as my childhood had been emotionally, I had never hurt badly enough to seek out a savior or surrender myself totally to another human being. And growing up with an authoritarian father, I was skeptical of people like the Maharishi Mahesh Yogi and Yogi Bhajan, who promoted themselves as Gurus with a capital G. (In a similar vein, I had always cringed in the presence of people who expected me to be subservient to them in their roles as Mentor, Coach, or Boss.) I was Guru-shy and Guru-averse. And my antipathy toward the idea of them—in the church, on the athletic field, and in the workplace—had only deepened as I had grown older.

My biggest beef with Gurus—and with authority figures and charismatic leaders in general—was how often they abused their power. Rajneesh, Yogi Bhajan, Muktananda, Sai Baba, Meher Baba, Bikram Choudhury—the list of Indian gurus who had been hypocritical, venal, and corrupt went on and on. Some collected fancy houses and cars. Others had sex with young girls and boys while they demanded celibacy from their followers. The more famous and powerful they got, the more paranoid they seemed to become, until they saw conspiracies against them and their doctrines everywhere.

Of course, it wasn't just Indian gurus who had violated their followers' sacred trust. Scientology's L. Ron Hubbard used confidential information to blackmail people he either feared or didn't like. Elizabeth Clare Prophet, the founder of the Church Universal Triumphant, stockpiled a huge arsenal of weapons near Yellowstone National Park in anticipation of an apocalypse that never came. Jim Jones of the Peoples Temple persuaded hundreds of his followers to commit mass suicide.

Traditionally in India, a guru is a teacher who dispels the darkness of ignorance and imparts knowledge and wisdom; he is a spiritual guide. There is no denying the fact that power has corrupted numerous spiritual leaders over the years, but by no means all of them. Was the fact that I was so skeptical of gurus a liability in terms of my own spiritual quest? All the guru talk among the kirtan wallahs unsettled me. If I couldn't devote myself to a guru, how could I ever succeed in devoting myself to God? It was a question I'd need to further ponder.

*　　*　　*

On the way home from Omega I spent an afternoon at Ananda, a yoga ashram across the Hudson River in Monroe, New York. I had heard about the ashram from a young man who was conducting workshops on the neuroscience of yoga. He told me that Nāda yoga, the form practiced at the ashram, originated in the first millennium B.C., when its yogis meditated on the mantra Om, the primordial sound of the universe, as a means of uniting with God and tuning their minds to align with the celestial, cosmic music vibrations. The young man described these early Nāda yogis as being the "first string theorists." (According to the string theory of modern physics, the universe is made up of infinitesimally small subatomic strands of energy vibrating at different frequencies and wavelengths.) He also told me that Ananda's founder had urged his students to meditate on one particular type of vibration—the persistent ringing sound that many people have in their ears. I was aware of a buzzing in my own ears that didn't seem generated by an outside source, but it wasn't very loud and it never lasted long enough to annoy me.

Only a handful of people were at the ashram that afternoon. But I stayed long enough to sit in on a class in Sanskrit, have a vegetarian lunch, and stroll around some of the ashram's eighty-five acres of woods and meadows. When I left, I also had in my possession a curious little book that had been written by the ashram's founder, Shri Brahmananda Sarasvati, a medical doctor and Sanskrit scholar who was dedicated to the integration of Eastern and Western sciences, culture, and philosophy. His book is titled *Nāda Yoga: The Science, Psychology and Philosophy of Anahata Nāda Yoga*. In it, Shri Brahmananda (who died in 1993) defined Nāda yoga as the "inner music of existence." He also referred to Nāda yoga as the "inner guru," or guide. Partly because the book was so short (only seventy-seven pages), I read it ten times over the next few days, as Shri Brahmananda had instructed his students to do in order to "assimilate" the spirit of the book. In the process, Nāda yoga became an unanticipated bridge between string theory and chanting for me. And it took me on the type of fascinating side trips you encounter when you go shopping for God.

I was particularly intrigued when Shri Brahmananda described Nāda yoga as "the voice of silence" and "as the union with the Self by means of the inner music and inner light." It reminded me of all those hours I had spent in the Morningside Meeting listening for my inner promptings from God: Could a person achieve the same results by meditating on the buzzing in their head?

I closed my eyes and waited until I perceived a ringing sound in my head, which took a while. "To some it may sound like the ocean's roar or water passing through pipes," Shri Brahmananda wrote. "Some may hear a sound like evening crickets or other vibrating insects; like the beat of a powerful, resonant drum; like tinkling bells or idling engines." To me, it was definitely those crickets, on a summer night, kind of a peaceful sound, faint. I spent several minutes using that sound as the focus for my meditation, and I achieved the same level of calm I'd experienced with other forms of meditation.

In his book, Shri Brahmananda refers to a medical condition called tinnitus. According to the American Tinnitus Association, an estimated fifty million American adults have tinnitus to some degree; of that number, approximately sixteen million have it severely enough to seek medical help. Tinnitus sufferers describe the buzzing, ringing, roaring, hissing, clicking, and other sounds it creates in their ears as annoying to varying degrees. Tinnitus is generally a symptom that something is wrong in the auditory system, including the ear, the auditory nerve, and the areas of the brain that process sound. Shri Brahmananda described tinnitus as being "nature's alarm clock . . . our telephone call coming long distance from heaven through our body and mind to alert us to pay attention to our inner life." The practice of meditating on the Nāda "refines the mind, heart and emotions of the meditator," he said, tuning the meditator's mind to the inner music of life. Although I wouldn't recommend Shri Brahmananda's meditation technique as a means of treating tinnitus, I definitely enjoyed trying it.

Neptune-ing Out

October Through February

When I walked through the door after the retreat, Pip and Mac were so excited to see me they almost knocked me down. Elizabeth and the kids were also happy to see me, but they were clearly much more focused on buying clothes and books and getting ready for the new school year.

After a weekend of dancing and singing and experiencing communal bliss, my quotidian home life felt like a bit of a letdown. And I didn't know what to do next concerning my spiritual quest. So, on the recommendation of a trusted friend, I made an appointment to see an astrologer named Faith Linda Weissman. My friend said that she would be sensitive to my spiritual aspirations and might have insights into the path ahead.

I had gone to astrologers before and, although I didn't swear by them or rely on them to make important decisions or plot the course of my life, I did find the best of them to be particularly intuitive and caring people who used the poetic and myth-infused language of astrology to help people like me move ahead in our lives.

We were sitting across from each other in a small, windowless room cooled by a softly whirring table fan. Faith Linda (as she preferred to be called) rented the room by the hour in a suite of other such rooms used by psychologists, psychics, and other itinerant healers. She was pretty, sixtyish, and trim—and bore a striking resemblance to the actress Audrey Hepburn in the later stages of her life and career. Like Hepburn, Faith Linda spoke with an indeterminate accent—was she Swiss, Polish, Dutch? I got the sense that she moved around a lot, perhaps from ashram to ashram, or holy place to holy place, I wasn't sure. She was a spiritual vagabond—ethereal, well meaning, and sweet.

By way of introduction, Faith Linda said, "We astrologers are half mathematicians—and half spiritual midwives and intuitive soul doctors." She described herself as a Western astrologer trained in the "complex and nuanced" Uranian system of astrology, which was founded in Hamburg, Germany, in the early 1920s.

I had given her my vitals—August 21, 1953, Cleveland, Ohio, 4:55 A.M.—when I called to make my appointment. Now she placed a copy of my natal chart in front of me. I grabbed it firmly, so the tiny desk fan wouldn't blow it away.

"You are heavily Leo. Because Leo is your rising as well as your birth sign, you are a Leo Leo, Lee," she told me, pointing to the notations she'd made in the margins of the chart. "The rising sign in the ancient world was considered even more of a mark of a person than their sun," she said. "It is the constellation that was rising in the heavens when you were born, and so it's the face you give spontaneously to the world and where you are intuitively yourself."

She moved from my rising sign to my sun sign. "You might

think of it as 'the egoic center of consciousness,' as the Jungians say. If you believe in reincarnation, as I assume you do—"

"I can't say that," I said. The truth was, I hadn't given reincarnation much thought beyond the psychological version of it that I'd taken away from Joe Loizzo's class. And I'd had absolutely no indication that I'd lived before or would live again after I died.

It was as if she hadn't heard me. "You've clearly been given a manifestation in this incarnation to work with your Leo energy," she went on. "Leo represents the king, the ruler, royalty. So there are lots of issues about wanting and needing to be seen, needing to be at the center of things, needing to be acknowledged in one's dignity, for one's gifts. The problem from a spiritual perspective," she said, "is that you don't want to identify with any of this. This is not the I Am. This is the provisional I Am, the personality I Am, the identity I Am for this incarnation. It is not the I Am."

By "I Am," did she mean the "Real Me," as opposed to my body and personality? Perhaps she was referring to the I Am that is one of the names for God in the Book of Exodus. I really wanted to know what she meant, but she was moving way too quickly for me to ask.

"As a Leo you must express all this but not identify with it," she was saying. "There will be people who won't want to read what you write—and this will frustrate you. It will have nothing to do with how good your writing is; it will have to do with the nature of the times and whether people are willing to receive your message."

She noted how Bach wasn't given his due until he was rediscovered after his death by Mendelssohn.

"The same will be true for your spiritual teachings," she said. "You will be denied recognition in your lifetime so that you can step back and do what you need to do without any attachment to the outcome."

Her comparison of me to one of the greatest artists who ever lived was silly, of course. But I did appreciate the silver lining she found in the likelihood that I'd never become famous—and how she elevated the significance of my small life by placing it into a larger generational context.

"All of us who were born between 1938 and 1956 are part of the Pluto-in-Leo generation," she said. "Our parents' Pluto-in-Cancer generation was all about the family, home, tribe, and nationality. Ours is about doing our own thing. We are reclaiming the Leo individuality—for ourselves but also for our culture."

"That's very interesting," I said. And I meant it. "But what I'd really like to know is how my family will be affected by my current spiritual quest. Do you have any sense of that?"

"Yes, I do," she said. "Mercury is rising in your chart. It is also seated on the north node of Neptune, the planet we associate with spiritual journeys. Neptune is really trying to express itself in your spiritual path. And Mercury, the god of dreams, the god we refer to as the psycho-compass, the god who takes the soul to the underworld, is your guide. Is that clear?"

"I think so."

"Now bear with me. Pluto is the great transformer. He determines how deeply we'll go in our journeys. You have a very nice aspect from Pluto to Saturn in your First House."

"What does that mean?" I asked.

"That there's a mandate for you to go on this journey . . . in this incarnation. No matter how difficult it is for you, no matter what it brings up in your life, you are being asked to go on this journey."

"And Elizabeth?" I wanted to know how my journey would impact my wife.

"What I first need to tell you is that everyone born between 1938 and 1956 has Saturn and Neptune in Libra, which is the sign of marriage. And that's a difficult signature for those of us who want to establish long-term relationships—it has caused a lot of disruption in people's lives. Neptune is idealistic about relationships and tends to idealize his partner, but he doesn't like too much responsibility. He kind of chafes at the bit. He wants to be able to disappear whenever he wants to." That sounded a lot like me.

"You have Saturn and Neptune on the fourth cusp. Now listen closely. Neptune, the god of the seas, likes being in vast, undifferentiated places. Chanting with Krishna Das, writing poetry, going to the movies: These are Neptune's ideas of a good time. Neptune is the inspirational portal because he doesn't like boundaries, he has this unbounded quality. We call it Neptune-ing out. But here he is with Saturn, who wants no part of that. Saturn says make a decision and stick with it, no matter what."

"And Elizabeth?"

"Your Saturn is on her Jupiter. She may be feeling shut out by your Neptune expansiveness."

I wasn't surprised. It made me sad to think that my quest for God was bringing such pain to the woman I loved. Should I pull my unbounded Neptune back to earth so that I could devote more time and energy to her?

Faith Linda believed that I should consider it.

"This is your second Saturn return," she explained. "It happens once every twenty-nine years, so it's a huge deal. Because your Saturn is in Libra, there will be demands on your marriage and home life. Saturn is asking you to give more of yourself to your family. They need you now. Your parents may be needing more of you, too."

"Is there anything else I should know?"

She mulled over my chart.

"Ah, this is interesting," she says. "There's a once-in-a-lifetime change in your lunar nature. You'll have a Pluto transit over the next two years. It will be a very emotional time for you. But it may also manifest itself in the women in your life. Elizabeth may undergo a rather intense change. Is there anything going on with her beyond your journey?"

"She's past her child-making years and that saddens her," I said. "So does the fact that Noah is almost as tall as she is. And Ben and Caroline will be driving soon, then going to college. Elizabeth loves being a mom but hates how it's all going by so quickly."

"How about your mother? Is there anything important going on with her? Where and when was she born?"

"In Cleveland," I say. "On March 15, 1932."

"Ah, the ides of March."

I told her about my mother's four herniated discs and recent cancer biopsy. "She's in a great deal of pain. Her friends are either dead or dying. She's afraid that she's getting Alzheimer's, which she isn't, but her mother got it, so she's convinced she will, which adds to her overall feeling that her life's not worth living. . . . And Caroline, the other important woman in my life, will turn sixteen next year."

Faith Linda smiled knowingly. "Enough said."

As I left Faith Linda, I kept repeating that one phrase in my mind: "Neptune-ing out." Over the past year, I had been fulfilling my desire to explore the vast, undifferentiated spaces of the soul, the spirit, whatever it is that people seek when they're looking for something more essential and true. But back on earth, on 110th Street and Riverside Drive, there was a family (and more particularly, two women) who needed more of me. As did a third woman—my mother, in Florida, who was in so much pain. Would I need to sacrifice my needs for theirs? Or was there a "Middle Way" that would allow me to stay on a spiritual path while being present and a source of strength to my loved ones? That was the question my "spiritual midwife," as Faith Linda called herself, nursed along.

Ever since my weekend at Omega, I had been urging Elizabeth to begin taking voice lessons. She finally agreed, and wondered if there was someone who'd take her on as a student at Bloomingdale, the same music school where Ben and Noah took violin lessons. At first she was shy about finding a teacher and wrote to the head of the school, a woman named Bathsheba: "I realize that your teachers are there to take talent and make it better. Do you think you have a teacher who would be willing to work with someone who is always off-key?"

Bathsheba recommended that Elizabeth interview two teachers: Molly, who she described as being "bubbly, energetic, and organized," and Nancy, who was "experienced, structured, and kind." She ended up choosing Molly, an opera singer who had studied at Carnegie Mellon and specialized in the music Elizabeth wanted most to sing: Broadway and pop standards.

Elizabeth had grown up in a musical family—she and her father were the only ones who couldn't carry a tune. Her brother Michael, who starred in all the high school musicals, let her know it. "I was told I was bad and always thought that singing was something you could never simply learn," she told Molly at their first lesson. "You could learn the piano but not singing."

Molly gave Elizabeth several exercises to test if she was tone-deaf; she wasn't. "You have a fine ear," Molly told her, "and a sophisticated sense of music."

For the next several months, Elizabeth met weekly with Molly for half an hour. They did ear training and vocal exercises and began by singing what Molly called "easy-ish" songs like "Baby Mine," from the Disney movie *Dumbo*, and "Getting to Know You" from *The King and I*. Molly would play the piano while Elizabeth sang. Elizabeth told me that the half hour she spent with Molly was her happiest of the week.

And yet she was still self-conscious about her singing. She was vulnerable to criticism, especially when she perceived it as coming from her brother Michael, who was also living in New York, or the kids. One day Caroline laughed while Elizabeth was practicing "I Didn't Know What Time It Was," a song by Richard Rodgers and Lorenz Hart, in the car. Elizabeth was inconsolable for days. She was convinced that Caroline (and by extension the rest of our kids) hated her voice and would never be able to see the progress she was making through her hard work. When I chastised Caroline for hurting her mother, she said, "I wasn't laughing at Mom. I was laughing at those silly lyrics."

It disturbed me deeply to see Elizabeth feel so much pain while undertaking a journey that had required so much courage from her. I hoped that someday she'd be able disarm her critics, both real and imagined, by ignoring them. In his book *The Music of Life: The Inner Nature and Effects of Sound*, Hazrat Inayat Khan, the Indian Sufi master, recounts the story of the Arabian Khalif Omar, who was so powerful that his mere presence was enough to make an assassin drop his dagger. When the assassin asked Omar the source of his power, Omar said, "My at-one-ment with God." By which he meant that he was "in tune with the Infinite, in harmony with the whole universe," according to Hazrat Inayat Khan. I didn't expect Elizabeth to be in harmony with the entire universe, but I did hope that she would learn to sing well enough to build the self-confidence she would need to quiet her inner, naysaying demons. And that she could enjoy herself when she sang in Bloomingdale's *Music Sharing Hour*, the annual showcase for adult students in May.

I had met a singing coach at Omega named Claude Stein, who had an international reputation for helping people like Elizabeth find their natural voice. It wasn't until November that I finally persuaded Elizabeth to see him. On a brisk fall day, we drove to Claude's home outside of Woodstock for the first lesson. His studio, in its own wing of the house, had a baby grand piano and a cathedral ceiling with impressive acoustics.

It was amazing how quickly Elizabeth shared her emotional pain with Claude.

"When they were younger," she said, "I used to sing to my kids all the time and they seemed to really love it. And then at a certain point they started to realize that Mom was really sort of sucky. And they started making fun of me. And it brought back the old hurts."

"Do you think Barbra Streisand asks a rap singer how she sounds?" he asked rhetorically. "You can always find people who don't think you sing well, and you can always find people who do like your voice. How do you feel the progress has been so far with your voice teacher? Be honest."

"There's been some successful ear training, but I don't see a huge difference," she said.

"What's that based on?" he asked.

"Just me hearing when it's good or bad. The tone, in particular, has not improved at all. It is unpleasant. It's just not pretty."

"Which means what? It's heavy? It's edgy? It's nasal?"

"It's just not pretty, even when I hit the right note. I hear myself sort of being good, then realize that I'm horrible. I'd like not to feel that I'm horrible."

"Spoken like a true dichotomous singer who thinks there's good and bad and off and on, rather than a professional singer who thinks, I'm a little flat today—two of the twelve notes were off—but the lyrics, the tone, and the message came through."

Then he summarized what he'd do for her. "I'll use every trick in my book to find the technique that works best with you. Some people respond better with external instructions about pitch, breath, and tone. I can do all that. But as we practice all those core competencies, I'll try to get you back to your original intention: what you really want to say with this song. And I'll try to make failure more acceptable to you, so that you can begin to deal with those feelings of shame."

There was a little bit of Buddha—or at least Joe Loizzo—in Claude's rap. He wanted to help Elizabeth become aware of her distorted perceptions and discover the compassionate teacher inside. And those were my wishes for Elizabeth, too. I wanted her to sing in the car or chant in yoga class without worrying how others would judge her. I wanted her to experience joy where there now was sadness. I wanted her to silence her inner music critic. Part of me thought that if Claude could help Elizabeth become more confident and adventurous as a singer, she'd accompany me on some of my spiritual journeys (at the very least the ones that involved singing), and I would feel less isolated and alone.

"All my weaknesses are in this one little singing box," she confessed.

"You're not alone," he said. "To avoid the embarrassment that comes with missing notes and being judged harshly, we end up developing bad habits and don't use our full vocal range. But it's amazing what happens in my workshop when you add a little relaxation into the mix. A shy person roars, an impatient person settles down, a jokester shows his vulnerability. It's very moving when a person expresses another part of himself. You can hear a pin drop, it's so powerful."

Claude was born in Jericho, Long Island. His father escaped Germany in 1939, right after Kristallnacht. Musical but mainly self-taught, as a child Claude took guitar lessons and was a drummer in his high school band. After graduating from Bard College, he went to New Orleans and started busking on street corners. Eventually he ended up in southern Florida, where his parents had moved, and played strip joints and bars before migrating back to New York.

The big turning point in his life came in 1983 when he took a course from a woman who taught actors to sing. He became her assistant and saw that he was good at what she did. One night he had a dream: "I was backstage at a Dylan concert, standing in line to get a book signed. When I got to him, Dylan said, 'You don't need a book.' His face transfigured into that of Jesus Christ, from on top of a mountain looking down on me and saying, 'It doesn't matter, Claude. You're on the path.'" Claude, who was twenty-four, had found his calling. He began giving classes and workshops in singing. His method evolved. Now, in addition to private coaching of the sort he was giving to Elizabeth, he held Natural Singer Workshops at retreats around the world, and increasingly for corporations seeking a fun way to raise their executives' performance and self-confidence.

"What kind of style appeals to you the most?" he asked Elizabeth.

"Standards. Jazz and Broadway. Also a little folk."

"And your favorite singers would be . . . ?"

"Ella Fitzgerald. Julie Andrews. And Peter, Paul and Mary."

"I'll correct you when you say negative things about yourself," he warned. "And I'll encourage you to be as positive as you can be. You hit a good note . . . and we break out the champagne."

He had asked her, before the session started, whether it was okay for me to watch. She had said yes, and now, on Claude's instructions, I was sitting quietly in a corner, taking notes on his technique.

He started with a song she already knew: "Getting to Know You." In B-flat. As he took her higher in terms of her range, she began hitting more of the notes. When Claude pointed that out, Elizabeth said, "But the tone was terrible."

Claude kept the focus on problem-solving, redirecting Elizabeth's negativity about the imperfections she heard. "I hear a little bit of edginess in this tone," he said. "But it's not terrible, and lip trills will loosen the tightness up. Now repeat after me: 'Piece of cake.'"

"Piece of cake," she sang.

"I don't give a damn."

"I don't give a damn," she repeated theatrically.

"Watch my lips."

"Watch my lips," she said, laughing.

"I can sing."

"I can sing. I can sing, I can sing," she sang in a faux-operatic voice.

Elizabeth was clearly starting to relax. Claude asked her to stand back a few feet and count whatever number of fingers he held up as she was singing. He explained, "I want to see if I can distract your mind even more."

"Drive a truck," he sang out.

"Drive a truck," she repeated. Claude flashed two fingers while she was singing. She called out, "Two."

Then he asked her to match her voice to whatever sequence of notes he started playing on the piano. After a few minutes he said, "That's a very complicated pattern we just did. You couldn't have succeeded in doing that if you didn't have a good ear. How did it feel to be so in the moment with your singing?"

"I felt like I was in a bubble," she said. Maybe this was what Joe Loizzo meant when he urged us to think of ourselves as a bubble of light and energy floating in a sea of bubbles during his Buddhism class: to be in the flow, the groove, the moment. When Elizabeth started singing "Getting to Know You" again, she seemed to be having a lot more fun.

"Beautiful," he said. "Now sit directly across from Lee and look into his eyes." Which she did. "No laughing," he instructed. "Just repeat after me."

"Thanks for listening," he sang.

"Thanks for listening," she repeated, looking self-consciously straight into my eyes.

"Thanks for caring."

"Thanks for caring," she sang.

"Now tell Lee why he means so much to you. Rather, sing it," he said.

"Because you are the father of my children," she sang. "Because you let me have my cats and dogs even though you're allergic." We all laughed.

Then Claude took over again.

"Because you cherish me."

"You cherish me," she sang.

"You know the music I am."

"You know the music I am."

"You want this dream for me."

At no point did she cry, which seemed to vex Claude. "You're not a big crybaby," he observed.

"Believe me," she said, "I've done my crying in my life. I have my share of things to cry about. But, no, I'm not a crier."

"That's one place we have to go," he said. "To see what happens to your tone and pitch when the part of your brain that's holding in the tears lets go."

Elizabeth knew better than anyone else what a tough customer she could be. "Have you ever had to give up on anybody?" she asked.

"I've dropped students, but there's only one person who constantly reverted to being off-key in the thirty thousand students I've taught in my thirty years of teaching. He had inner ear damage. Oh, yes, and there was this one girl who couldn't stay on-key for 'Twinkle, Twinkle.'"

"I'm not in that category," she said.

"No, you're not." He laughed. "You have a strong will and an alert mind. And this is a good fire to walk through if you've got the balls to do it."

"I do," she said, laughing. "All my friends are, like, 'Oh, you're so brave, you're so brave.' And I'm, like, 'What's so brave about wanting to sing?'"

"What's brave is how you've faced your fears," Claude said. "And if weeping doesn't help you sound even better, we'll do something else. We'll juggle, we'll play catch, we'll do Donald Duck voices."

Then he directed Elizabeth and me to sing to each other. Until that moment, I had been a silent observer, feeling particularly impressed with how Claude had gotten Elizabeth to take risks and try on new voices as she looked for her own. Wasn't I doing the same thing as I searched for a spiritual identity and home? I kept taking risks and trying on new traditions and practices, in the hope that one or more of them would lead me to the spiritual home I had longed for. But strangely, when Claude invited me to become an active participant in Elizabeth's voice lesson, my first instinct was to back off. It was probably the same instinct Elizabeth had whenever I asked her to join me for a workshop or religious service related to my spiritual quest. A sense that "It's your thing, not mine," perhaps. Or the way we as humans tend to push away (at first) when someone tries to pull us in their direction.

Claude had tried to pull me into Elizabeth's voice lesson, and at first I'd pushed the idea away. But now I joined willingly.

"I will listen," I sang, following Claude's cue.

"I will hear you," I sang, looking into Elizabeth's eyes.

Claude asked Elizabeth if she was aware of feeling anything.

"I'm feeling a lot of gratitude," she said. She wasn't very convincing. But then again, she was doing just what I would have done: trying to please her teacher. She was also cloaking herself in the feeling of gratitude as part of the process of truly experiencing and embracing it.

"So tell him," Claude ordered.

"Thank you . . . thank you, my dear husband," she sang. "I've never felt loved so much."

"Now tell him what you'll do for him," he said.

"I'll do anything for you, dear, anything, for you, dear, anything, for you," she sang. She hadn't shed a single tear; nor had she fully connected with the emotion of gratitude yet. But she was hitting more notes and singing with more feeling: She was on her way.

Krishna Meets Radha

March Through May

At the end of March, Omega held its annual Spring Ecstatic Chant weekend, which featured fewer big-name stars. My great discovery of the weekend was a kirtan wallah by the name of Shyamdas. He seemed like a person of uncommon depth and commitment. Also, he made me laugh—in the earthy, straight-from-the-belly way that I imagined Borscht Belt comedians once made my grandparents roar at the nearby Catskill resorts.

Shyamdas looked a bit like Ringo Starr. He was avuncular, with a short-cropped gray beard and hair, and there was something refreshingly authentic about him: He wore a loose-fitting, collarless shirt that fell to his knees, and moved his head back and forth in a figure eight, the way Indians do when they listen to music or gesture accha (the word for "good" or "I understand" in Hindi). At particularly ecstatic points in a chant, Shyamdas would punch his arm into the air and flick his fingers toward the sky, showing his delight in the pleasure the music was giving to him, the audience, and the gods. "The main thing is to literally sing your heart out," he said. "So that all the love in your heart is manifested in the world."

At times, after he'd been riffing and scatting, Shyamdas would seem to fall asleep, or drift off, for a while, before snapping back to attention. "It's about forgetting who we are for the time being," he said of kirtan. "That's what ecstatic chanting is all about."

He was born Stephen Theodore Schaffer in New Haven, Connecticut, in 1953, the same year I was born. He was raised Jewish but didn't have a bar mitzvah. In the early 1970s he read Ram Dass's *Be Here Now* and felt the same generational pull that led Jai Uttal and Krishna Das to India, where he ended up studying classical Indian music, Sanskrit, and half a dozen regional Indic languages.

He became a disciple of Neem Karoli Baba, then Shri Goswami Prathameshji, taking up residence in Vrindavan, the town in northern India where the flute-playing Lord Krishna was said to have spent his childhood dancing with the local gopis, or cow-herding girls. As a temple kirtan singer, he became known for weaving together songs, stories, and bhakti teachings in the spirit of the ancient ecstatic bards.

Then, in the 1980s, Shyamdas started making yearly trips to the United States to lead kirtan at yoga centers and retreats like the one we were currently at.

On this afternoon he was sharing the stage with his equally accomplished friend Radhanath Swami, who had been born Richard Slavin, in Chicago, three years before Shyamdas and I were born. Slavin had spent his early twenties wandering as an ascetic in northern India. Then he, too, ended up in Vrindavan, where he joined the International Society of Krishna Consciousness and took the monastic vows of a Vaishnava sannyasin. For nearly thirty years, Radhanath Swami had been guiding an ashram in Mumbai that delivered vegetarian food to children in the city's slums; he had been honored for his humanitarian work all over the world. But what struck me, at Omega, was his playfulness and sense of humor. With his shaved head and gentle smile, Radhanath Swami looked like and had the energy of someone half his age.

When he joined Shyamdas for a set, Radhanath Swami put his hands together and bowed to us, humbly asking if he could lead us in the sacred Om. As he said Om, the tremor in his voice was like that of a cantor chanting the Kol Nidre at the start of Yom Kippur. We all joined in, and the hall vibrated from wall to wall and floor to rafters. Then he asked if we would like to hear a story about Krishna and Radha and their childhood in Vrindavan. That story led to another story, then another. Each time he finished a story, he asked, "Would you like to hear another story?" as if he were addressing a class of eager-eyed seven-year-olds. How could we say no?

"The source of all love in bhakti is the love of Radha for Krishna," he finally said. "The fundamental need we have as human beings is to love or be beloved."

Then he and Shyamdas started to intone the most venerated of all Hindu chants: the sixteen-word Hare Krishna Maha Mantra (or Great Mantra) of "Hare Krishna, Hare Krishna / Krishna, Krishna, Hare, Hare / Hare Rama, Hare Rama / Rama, Rama / Hare, Hare."

While "Krishna" and "Rama" are different names for God, "Hare" is the vocative of Radha, whose endless and unconditional love for Krishna is the one that exemplifies the deepest and most spontaneous love possible. "Hare" is also described as the divine feminine energy of the Lord, which gives the Maha Mantra its essential, revivifying sensuality. As one eighteenth century teacher famously wrote, "When the sixteen names and thirty-two syllables of the Hare Krishna mantra are loudly vibrated, Krishna dances on one's tongue."

According to Steven J. Rosen, author of *The Yoga of Kirtan*, the Maha Mantra contains all the major spiritual sound vibrations. At the same time, it is Hinduism's anthem of selfless devotion. Quoting Krishna in the Bhagavad Gita, Radhanath Swami said, " 'If one offers me a single flower leaf or fruit with devotion, I will accept it.' " It had been the theme of each of his stories that afternoon: "When we offer selfless love to the Lord, the Lord accepts it. This divine love is within the heart of every living thing—and kirtan awakens it."

As the pace quickened and I got up to dance in the back of the hall, I experienced how the Maha Mantra could move the chanter further and further away from the mundane, material world toward union with the Divine. In the mindlessness and abandon of my dancing, I felt like a rocket that could blast off at any second toward the moon. By the time I sat back down, my head was spinning, so I slowed down my breathing and centered myself. When I looked up, the people still chanting and dancing had morphed into a sea of huge, exuberant smiles. I felt happy to be among them, and truly grateful. "The path of bhakti is tuning our consciousness into the infinite grace of the Lord," Radhanath Swami explained later. "We can only do that when we have willing and grateful hearts."

Had I been chanting out of devotion to God? I didn't think so. Still, I felt transformed by the experience. Part of that feeling could be attributed to changes that had taken place in my body and brain. A recent study by nine Swedish neuroscientists determined that when people sing songs in unison, their heart rates synchronize so that they slow down and speed up at the same time. The same is true when people sing mantras in unison. Another study, by psychologist Robin Dunbar and his colleagues at the University of Oxford, reported that people who play music together have a higher tolerance for pain—an indication that their bodies are producing endorphins, a form of natural opiate. The same is not true of people who are simply listening to music. Dunbar also found that the pain threshold for members of a charismatic-type religious group that participated in a service that involved "communal singing, accompanied by clapping and a great deal of upper body movement" was higher than that of a group of people at an Anglican prayer meeting that didn't involve music. Other studies have shown that people who sing or move in rhythmic unison tend to work more cooperatively with each other and that performing music together builds empathy.

So, on a neurochemical level, it's not surprising that chanting had lifted my mood and connected me physically and emotionally to the people around me.

Radhanath Swami said, "The love of God is in every person's heart." It reminded me of the core Quaker belief: "There is that of God in everyone." Shyamdas added, "You can't love God and not love every human being, dog, cow, or elephant." I had been feeling that, too, expanding my circle of compassion beyond cats and dogs to include other animals, like horses, monkeys, and even spiders. Radhanath Swami summed up the spirit of the session by saying, "Nothing pleases Krishna more than the spirit of our compassion for others."

He told us a story about a woman who lived in a village near Mumbai. The village had been devastated by a terrible drought, and the woman asked Radhanath Swami to take her ten-year-old son to live in the orphanage he ran in Mumbai. "Before we left, she told me, 'Don't give my son anything for nothing. I don't want him to be a beggar. I want him to be grateful for all he earns.'"

Sometime later, Radhanath Swami received a sack of peanuts from the woman, their shells still caked in dirt. "The woman had walked miles each day to water the peanuts," he explained, "and now she was sending me the first ones she'd picked to thank me for taking care of her son. Those peanuts were more precious to me than diamonds and rubies. When I tasted them they were like nectar. You see, things don't make us happy," he said. "It's the love in the offering—the bhakti—that touches the heart." I wanted to keep that idea in mind as I tried to temper my tendency to Neptune out, and give my loved ones the support they might need in the months ahead.

According to Sri Chaitanya, bhakti, the continuous love of God, is the natural condition of the soul and leads to eternal, enlightened bliss. I got a glimpse of that bliss in the delight that Radhanath Swami took in the peanuts—and in that way that he and Shyamdas were always trying to find new ways to sing Krishna's praises and keep the ancient mantras fresh. You sensed that the two friends would never tire of Krishna, or the human capacity for love.

In an interview with Steven J. Rosen that I found particularly interesting, Shyamdas talked about "the existential theological question" he faced before his first trip to India: "Was Brahman, or Absolute Reality, nirguna or saguna? That is to say, in the ultimate analysis, is God without qualities and impersonal, or is He the Supreme Person, full of ecstatic qualities?" After considerable internal debate, he chose saguna over nirguna and made Krishna his personal Lord.

At the beginning of my own journey, when I took the Belief-O-Matic quiz, I understood God to be "the impersonal Ultimate Reality which resides within and/or beyond all." During the past year I had discovered how hard it was to grow more spiritually connected to a life force, cosmic order, or impersonal Ultimate Reality. Abstractions hurt my brain and left me numb. I realized it would be much more likely for me to experience gratitude, awe, and love in relationship to a personal deity, even if that deity were a confabulation. Shyamdas helped me clarify that dilemma—to understand the choice I had between nirguna and saguna, the impersonal and the personal, going forward. By letting a little Krishna, Jesus, and saguna into my life, by allowing myself to praise God, chanting one or more of his thousand different names, I was much more likely to feel compassion for the rest of humanity, and act more lovingly toward my parents, children, and wife.

Back in New York, I had one more session with Faith Linda, the astrologer. I wanted to zero in on where my spiritual quest was and where it might be headed. I began by asking her to tell me about her own spiritual life.

"I was born Jewish and spent a lot of my life practicing Zen Buddhism," she said. "Now I'm part of the Jewish Renewal movement. Do you know what that is? Whenever I'm in the city I try to go to Romemu, this new Renewal congregation. Its rabbi is also an astrologer."

I told her that I had been hearing about Romemu a lot lately, from people like her who identified themselves as "seekers." From what I had heard, Romemu incorporated many of the elements of prayer I'd been exploring lately—meditation, call-and-response chanting, and yoga. "It's only a few blocks away from my apartment," I added. "I want to try a Friday night service there."

"Yes, do that," she said. "But if you really want to learn about Jewish Renewal, find an opportunity to meet Reb Zalman, the cofounder of the movement. He lives in Boulder, Colorado, where he holds the wisdom chair at Naropa University." She added, "He's eighty-eight and in poor health, so it's important that you see him soon."

"With all your traveling and Zen, isn't it strange to be so involved with Judaism again?" I asked her.

"Not at all," she said. "We're incarnated in this life as Jews, so being Jewish has this meaning for us that we need to explore. Many of the great teachers in India understand that. They will tell their Western students to go home and go back to their own tradition."

I still didn't relate to the reincarnation part of what Faith Linda was saying, but I did see her other point—that it might be easier to find meaning in the religion in which I was raised.

"But if I go back to Judaism and explore it in a deeper way, I still face a huge problem," I said. "Elizabeth and I have very different ideas about spirituality. She's an atheist and I'm searching for God. I'll keep Neptune-ing out, at the risk of alienating my family and feeling increasingly alone."

"People on the spiritual path begin by adding it on to their life—it's just a side dish at first. But if you're seriously on the spiritual path, it changes your relationship to everything," she said. "You become radically altered and your spiritual life becomes the main meal. That's where the conflict really comes in." This sparked my deepest fear: that my family would get sick of me, or I'd end up leaving them behind.

Elizabeth's big day finally arrived. Earlier that week she had practiced her scales and lip trills considerably more than usual and taken an extra lesson with Molly. She made a large pitcher of sangria, to be shared later that afternoon with the two friends she'd invited to the showcase. The kids dressed in nice clothes and I put on a sport jacket. Then we walked two blocks to the Bloomingdale School of Music and took seats close to the front of the first-floor performance room.

The showcase was called *Music Sharing Hour*. The first performer, a middle-aged violinist with sleek silver hair, played his two songs—the Siciliano from Bach's "Violin Sonata No. 1 in G minor" and Beethoven's "Joyful, Joyful We Adore Thee"—quite competently for a beginner. Another violinist followed with a halting but charming Boccherini's "Minuet." Then it was Elizabeth's turn. Dressed in a brown chiffon gown, she walked up to the music stand. With Molly accompanying her on the piano, she sang two songs: Rodgers and Hart's "It's Easy to Remember" and George and Ira Gershwin's "Embraceable You." Elizabeth didn't hit all the notes, but she certainly hit more than any of us expected—and her theatricality, which had bothered our kids in her early, less confident days, really added to her spirited performance. None of the kids giggled or rolled their eyes, and when she was done, we all applauded wildly. We were proud of her. Elizabeth had faced her deepest fears and not let the naysayers in her life keep her from chasing her dream. She had done well, and felt good about it. Time to break out the sangria.

part four

Season of Community and Renewal

Love Yah, who is your God,
in what your heart is, in what you aspire to,
in what you have made your own.
—Reb Zalman Schachter-Shalomi

Membership and Manna

June Through March

When Katherine's husband told us that she had been diagnosed with Stage 2 breast cancer—and that she would be having surgery the following week—we were deeply concerned. From our experience with other friends, we knew that Katherine would be facing emotional ups and downs during her treatment—for instance, in a few weeks she'd be mourning the loss of her thick auburn hair. Elizabeth marched right up to Katherine's apartment with a pair of barber shears and a bottle of wine and gave her a short, stylish haircut that lifted up Katherine's spirit. That Sunday, at the Bulls Head–Oswego Meeting I attended near our home in upstate New York, I asked the sixteen Quakers gathered there to hold Katherine in the Light. It was the first time I had done anything like that in more than a year of attending meetings, so I emailed her about it.

"That is so wonderful and kind," she wrote back. "It must be working," she added, "since I am feeling strong and ready for this journey."

I wasn't the only person who had asked for Katherine to be held in the Light that day. Katherine herself had asked the Morningside Meeting to do the same. When she did, no one said anything; instead, true to Quaker etiquette, they simply listened and took in Katherine's words. Then, during the hospitality hour, a black woman with a gray buzz cut walked over to within a few feet of her. "Georgette didn't say anything," Katherine told me. "She had no pity or platitudes to offer me. The look in her eyes simply said, *You're going to go through something really hard. And you'll be able to count on me.*"

Georgette and two other women formed an unofficial "Committee for Katherine." It was understood that they would help her with whatever she might need—rides, companionship, support. One of the women put the exact times of Katherine's chemotherapy appointments in her date book, so that she could hold Katherine in the Light during those hours. "That small gesture was so simple and human," Katherine said. "It meant the world to me." During the most grueling period of her chemotherapy, the Committee for Katherine asked to meet with her. "We didn't say anything. We just sat in the small room off the main meeting hall. And yet, I felt cleansed and refreshed when I left. It was unbelievable. That small room had become a sacred place of healing for me."

Her six months of treatment killed "every cell in my body," Katherine said. But the unconditional love she received from the members of the Meeting nurtured her hope that, by springtime, she would be "born anew" with the budding flowers. She had starting thinking more and more about officially becoming a Quaker. In a pamphlet on membership, the Quaker writer Leonard S. Kenworthy wrote, "Our society is not one of saints but of seekers, yearning for Divine Guidance in their lives and in the world around us." I couldn't see Katherine ever yearning for Divine Guidance—"the God and Christ stuff," as she called it, still bugged her—but she had come to embrace many of Quakerism's core principles and practices. Kenworthy also described membership as "a learner's permit for the life-long journey towards truth and fulfillment." I could certainly see Katherine subscribing to that.

Over the next few weeks, the Committee for Katherine helped her address her lingering concerns about becoming a Quaker. Then, in October, Katherine became an official member of the Morning-side Meeting. She described it to me in an email:

"There was no ceremony, no party, no hoopla. Just like any other Sunday, we sat in silence. Then a woman stood up to quote the nature writer Wendell Berry. A man said something about the sacred obligation Quakers have to seek harmony as an antidote to the divisiveness caused by corporate greed. Then one of the members of the Committee for Katherine said that she was delighted to announce that I had become a member of the Meeting. I said 'Yay!' and then some words I don't remember. After the meeting, I spent a few minutes talking with Ned, who had just gotten a heart transplant. OMG! A new heart! You've got to see a message for me in that!"

I was happy for Katherine. She had found a spiritual home—a community of caring individuals who shared her values and principles, who would support her in good times and bad, who would help her evolve spiritually and give her a base for advocating the causes and ideals that mattered most to her. In retrospect, of course, it seemed that Katherine and the Morningside Meeting were made for each other. She wasn't a birthright Quaker, but she had gone to Quaker schools and internalized enough Quaker values to want her daughter Abigail to attend a Quaker school as well. When she encountered a moral or psychological challenge—9/11, her mother's dementia, her own breast cancer—Katherine looked to the silence and camaraderie of Friends meetings for strength and perspective. When she visited the Morningside Meeting for the first time, during the Gulf War, she said that it felt like "coming home." It was only natural that she commit to becoming a Quaker there.

By contrast, there was nothing in my own DNA or background that made Quakerism an inevitable sangha for me. I liked and had enormous respect for the people I met at the Morningside and Bulls Head–Oswego Meetings, but each time I went there I felt like an outsider, a tourist, someone with one foot out the door.

I had felt similarly about the communities at Nalanda and Omega. In the ten weeks of classes I took at Tibet House, the Four Noble Truths took me deeper into myself; they didn't build a sense of fellowship in me. A different dynamic was at play during the weekends I spent chanting with Krishna Das and the other kirtan wallahs. Vibrating in unison with them—to the point of synchronizing heart rhythms—I felt a primal kinship with my fellow chanters. Then, out of nowhere, something would squelch my desire to bond further. For example, one evening, after sitting in a half-lotus position for an hour, I stretched into a much more comfortable V with my legs. The woman next to me gave me a dirty look. "You can't sit like that," she said sternly. "Why?" I asked. "Because you're being disrespectful to the artists and their music." It was apparently a cardinal sin in this particular tradition to show your feet to a person who deserved your respect. So I shifted back into the half lotus, and the evening was ruined for me.

The next day, when Shyamdas took center stage, a man who looked to be in his late twenties shouted, "We love you, Shyamdas!"

It was the same behavior I'd seen at a dozen rock concerts. "We love you, Jackson!" "We love you, Bruce!" Even though I absolutely adored Shyamdas's artistry and respected him deeply, what right did this young man have to speak for me and everyone else in the room? And wasn't the whole weekend about loving and getting closer to God, not Shyamdas, Radhanath Swami, or anyone else? At the end of the day, despite my enjoyment of kirtan, I couldn't get past the overlay of rules and guru worship in this particular community; nor did I like the fact that the front row at these ecstatic chant weekends seemed reserved for an inside circle of others who had made Osho or Maharaj-ji the center of their lives. I may have been wrong or misguided in these impressions, but I couldn't imagine being a member of a community that cared so much about how I crossed my legs. Or one that attracted so many groupies shouting out their love from the back and middle rows.

And yet, I yearned to be part of a community. I wanted a spiritual home, a place where I'd feel safe, nurtured, and supported as I looked for God. Like Katherine, I had never been a joiner. From nursery school until I graduated college, I always sat in the back of the class, where teachers were least likely to call on me. I played on all sorts of sports teams, but I never felt like one of the guys. I had a diverse group of friends. But I never felt compelled to join a fraternity or another group. I was more comfortable in situations where I could sneak out and keep a safe distance. Perhaps that was one of the main reasons I chose a profession that enabled me to report and write about a variety of worlds without becoming a card-carrying member of any one of them. Spiritually, however, it seemed that I would need a single home if I wanted to evolve. For that reason, something the astrologer Faith Linda Weissman had said intrigued me: "We're incarnated in this life as Jews, so being Jewish has this meaning for us that we need to explore." After all my forays into other traditions, I was beginning to conclude that it might be easier for me to find both meaning and a spiritual community in the religion to which I was born.

Faith Linda had sent me a link for an annual conference of Jewish "seekers" that would be taking place in Kerhonkson, New York, on the weekend of the Martin Luther King Jr. Day holiday. The four-day retreat would cost several hundred dollars I didn't have to spare, but because I lived in the area, I qualified for a one-day rate of $125. I chose Sunday, and got there as early as I could to get the most for my money.

The Catskills resort where the conference was held had seen much better days. Its lobby smelled like the swimming pool and locker room areas of an old YMCA. But there was something genuine—and even uplifting—about the setting. I was touched by the sight of men in yarmulkes and women in long skirts lounging on the couches with their kids; the makeshift booths that promoted Eco-Judaism, travel to Israel, a dozen synagogues and causes; the energized young people of every denomination and sexual orientation sharing their latest passion or idea.

"Limmud," the name of the conference, meant "learning" in Hebrew. The goal was to offer the seven hundred or so attendees "different points of connections to Jewish life—intellectual, spiritual, emotional, familial, and communal." A sampling of the dozens of workshops offered on Sunday included ones on Israeli folk dancing, a Jewish approach to organ donation, Jewish culinary history, dealing with loss and grief, and teaching Torah to your kids.

I was drawn to some of the quirkier sessions. The first I attended was called "Googling God: How the Internet Influences Our Image of God." Its stated purpose was to "put together a profile of God using the world's most powerful Internet search engine" and to "discuss ways in which we may alter that 'profile' to enhance our personal relationship with the Holy."

"How I Became a Jew," the second session I attended, featured a short, intense, and very muscular man who talked about his unlikely transformation from Louis Ferrante, a Gambino associate accused of masterminding some of the largest heists in history, into Moshe ben Abraham, observant Jew.

After that, I went to "The Forbidden Tree of Knowledge: Psychedelics and the Bible," led by a thirty-two-year-old social activist named Daniel Sieradski. Like me, Sieradski was interested in how neuroscience had begun mapping "the God circuitry" of the human brain. At the same time, he had done considerable research into the ritualized use of psychedelic drugs to achieve higher consciousness.

Sieradski began his lecture by repeating the familiar speculation that Moses, the Apostle Paul, Muhammad, Joan of Arc, and Joseph Smith were all epileptics—and that the hallucinations they experienced during seizures left them with a feeling of being "an emissary of the Divine." He noted how Dr. Michael Persinger, a neuroscientist at Laurentian University in Ontario, Canada, claimed to have achieved similar results in the 1980s with a helmet he designed that sent an electromagnetic field across the brain, stimulating the right parietal lobe and what Persinger called a "sensed presence of the divine." (To date, Persinger's findings have not been replicated.)

The main focus of Sieradski's talk was writer Terence McKenna's Stoned Ape theory of human evolution. In his book *Food of the Gods*, McKenna speculates that *Homo erectus*, our earliest ancestors, evolved into *Homo sapiens* about a hundred thousand years ago because they ate psychoactive psilocybin mushrooms as part of their diet. (Recent experiments have shown that psilocybin improves the visual acuity of humans; hence, nibbling on "magic" mushrooms might have helped our primate ancestors hunt more effectively and want more sex, resulting in more offspring and greater genetic diversity.) McKenna believed that these mushroom-nibbling ancestors had ecstatic visions that elicited a feeling of oneness and connection with everything around them. These same visions, he said, inspired the foundational myths of the world's earliest religions.

According to Sieradski, it was only a small leap from McKenna's Stoned Ape theory to author Dan Merkur's belief that all of the great religious mysteries—including the Burning Bush of the Exodus story—stemmed from the use of psychoactive drugs. In his book *The Mystery of Manna: The Psychedelic Sacrament of the Bible*, Merkur theorizes that the manna of the Exodus story contained a psychoactive fungus called ergot. After Moses fed the Israelites manna, "They looked toward the wilderness, and behold, the glory of Yahweh appeared in a cloud" (Exodus 16:10). Merkur believes that the first Christian Eucharist resulted from a similar psychedelic rite.

I got the impression that had it been legal, Sieradski would have passed around psilocybin mushrooms for us to examine and ingest. Instead, he ended his presentation by proposing that the Jewish holiday of Purim (which encourages Jews to make noise, wear costumes, and go crazy) include a rite of rabbinically sanctioned shroom taking.

In several of the sessions I attended, including Sieradski's, the underlying theme was how to get closer to the Divine. The music at Limmud was meant to help us get there. It was soulful, hip, and spiritual—and it drew on a rich variety of musical idioms and genres. The Kirtan Rabbi, Andrew Hahn, led call-and-response and participatory chanting with short, sacred phrases from the Jewish tradition. The Jazz Rabbi, saxophonist Greg Wall, had performed with such groups as Hasidic New Wave and the Later Prophets. Grammy-nominated trumpeter Frank London had played with the Klezmatics, LL Cool J, and They Might Be Giants, reinforcing the fact that this was not my parents' Judaism.

By the time Rabbi David Ingber arrived for his session, it was standing room only. Ingber clearly had his fans, including several young yeshiva types who were poised at the edge of their chairs, anxious to debate the finer points of Torah with him.

His session was called "Entering the Dark Cloud: Dealing with Obstacles in Spiritual Practice." I came, in part, to see whether I liked Ingber's style and way of thinking enough to visit Romemu, the synagogue he'd founded in my neighborhood. Also, I hoped that he would be addressing some of the challenges I'd been facing as I tried to balance my midlife spiritual search with my obligations to my family.

The forty-something Ingber had a weight lifter's body—broad shoulders, big chest, huge hands. He reminded me most of Mario Cuomo, the Jesuit-educated Italian-American Catholic who was once the governor of New York. Like Cuomo, Ingber obviously loved to read and sprinkled his opinions with quotes from philosophers and holy men. He had a ferocious, quick-witted intelligence, as well as an easy, compassionate smile.

He introduced the session by reading a passage from the Torah. I followed along on the copy I'd picked up when I walked into the session.

Exodus 20:18: "When the people saw the thunder and lightning and heard the trumpet and saw the mountain in smoke, they trembled with fear. They stayed at a distance." 19: "And they said to Moses, 'Speak to us yourself and we will listen. But do not have God speak to us or we will die.'" 20: "Moses said to the people, 'Do not be afraid. God has come to test you, so that the fear of God will be with you to keep you from sinning.'" 21: "The People remained at a distance, while Moses approached the thick darkness where God was."

The passage describes the moments before God revealed the Ten Commandments to Moses. To frame this snippet of Torah, Ingber read what various sages had written about it in the Zohar, the foundational work in the literature of Jewish mystical thought.

The sages were most interested in the contrast between how Moses and the Jewish people reacted to the dark cloud: While the people "remained at a distance," Moses approached "the thick darkness where God was." Ingber pointed out how the words "darkness" and "hindrance" share the same three letters in Hebrew. Hasidic Rebbe Nachman of Bratslav (1772–1810) had used that fact to explain that "G-d actually hides G-d's self in the hindrance." He wrote, "One who is aware . . . more mindful, can find G-d in the midst of the hindrances themselves."

Reading Exodus when I was a kid—and even as a young adult—I didn't heed how the Jewish people reacted to the dark cloud. It merely passed me by, subsumed by the supernatural encounter between Moses and God, which left me incredulous. But now, at Limmud, with its emphasis on new learnings, I felt encouraged to take a second look. Rebbe Nachman had used Buddha-like language to describe the search for God. And the young rabbi who reminded me of Mario Cuomo was urging me to weigh the personal relevance of what Nachman had said.

Like the Jews in the desert, my own tendency had been to stay away from the darkness and keep my distance from the God of the Torah. That God was angry and jealous; I couldn't picture him; I didn't feel compelled to praise or emulate him or give him any credit for the sunset that wowed me or the awe I felt when my children were born. As my yearning for God grew, I didn't look to the Torah; I looked to Jesus, the Buddha, and Krishna.

What the Zohar seemed to be saying was: Don't keep going in so many directions; give the God of the Torah a chance. Maybe he's buried somewhere in all those hindrances that have caused you to turn your back on him, in those biblical texts where he seemed to slaughter whole cities and drown entire generations on a whim.

"We live in a generation that has post-traumatic God disorder," Ingber said, as if he were reading my mind. "We have difficulty dealing with a God who has a dark side. But the Zohar says that you need darkness to show the light; you need folly to show wisdom. In other words, wisdom doesn't exist without folly. When we are in a dark place, confronted by an unknown and unknowable terror, the one who steps inside can get revelation."

It could have been Joe Loizzo talking—or the Buddha. "When pain or darkness arises, lean into it," Ingber was saying. Then he closed his eyes and took a deep breath. "Just breathe into the fear."

It had been way too easy for me to dismiss my birthright religion as having nothing to offer me spiritually. And so I had gone on a long pilgrimage to find in other traditions the spiritual nourishment that was lacking for me in Judaism. Along the way, I had met dozens of similarly disaffected Jews, including some who had taken Hindu, Buddhist, or Sufi names. I didn't think badly of them for abandoning their birthright faith; indeed, they were kindred spirits and fellow seekers, and some of them, like Shyamdas and Krishna Das, had helped people like me heal their wounds and open their hearts.

Unlike the seekers who had left Judaism, Ingber treated his birthright religion as "a toolbox for spiritual growth." He looked to the great Jewish mystics who lived in twelfth century Spain and southern France and in eighteenth century Eastern Europe for inspiration. He was a scholar of the Torah whose goal was to "juice the texts for that which is nutritious," he said. At the same time, he used meditation and ecstatic chanting and dancing to get closer to the Divine. The rabbis at my childhood synagogue seemed most comfortable in business suits; I sensed that this rabbi, who was at the forefront of the movement called Jewish Renewal, was happiest in his bare feet, davening like a madman and dancing up a storm.

A month after Limmud, I took off from our apartment on West 110th Street at 6:00 P.M. on a Friday evening, and walked two blocks east and five blocks south to the corner of Amsterdam and West 105th Street, where Romemu leased space in the West End Presbyterian Church. It took me exactly seven minutes to get there.

As I walked up the stairs and into the church, a volunteer usher wished me a "gut Shabbos" and directed me to a pile of mimeographed siddurim, or prayer books, on a back table. I picked one up, then took a seat in the last row.

The chairs started filling up at around 6:25 P.M. Although there were men and women who wore business suits, most were dressed more comfortably, in everything from jeans and yoga clothes to hippie attire. A surprising number of women wore long skirts and had their heads covered. Maybe half the men were wearing yarmulkes, in a variety of colors; the rest covered their heads with berets, base-ball caps, embroidered hats, and fedoras. I had on a standard-issue black yarmulke I'd gotten at a wedding. Looking around the church, I made a rough estimate that there were slightly more than three hundred worshippers there. About a third of them were in their twenties and thirties; another third looked my age or older.

Rabbi Ingber stood at the front of the church, behind the sturdy bimah, or pulpit. There was an ark holding the Torah behind him, and a group of musicians standing several feet to his right. As people continued to come in, he began humming a niggun, or wordless melody. I couldn't tell whether he was singing, "Lai, lai, lai" or "Dai, dai, dai" or "Yai, yai, yai," or something altogether different, but the effect, particularly when the guitarist and drummer joined in, and the worshippers, too, was beautiful and comforting.

I scanned the siddur. It had been put together by Rabbi Marcia Prager, the leader of a Renewal congregation in Philadelphia. In "'Naming' God," her introduction to the siddur, she wrote that "the Hebrew letters יהוה constitute the unpronounceable four-letter name of God which subsumes and unites all descriptions which Jewish tradition has evolved in our quest for the Divine." (יהוה, the inexpressible name of God, is generally transliterated as YHVH and traditionally pronounced as "Adonai," meaning "Lord," when in-voked in prayer.) There are no vowels in יהוה, so the aspirate conso-nants that make up the word can only be pronounced by breathing. For that reason, she wrote, the Renewal community translates the Divine Name יהוה into English as "the Breath of Life." You could substitute other God-names when you came upon יהוה in the siddur, including Endless One, Fountain of Blessing, or Source of All Life. But keep in mind, she stressed, that "יהוה hints at the absurdity of assigning a name to an ineffable Divinity."

I really liked that Prager tackled the issue of God's name up front. In the siddur I used growing up, God was continually being referred to as "the Lord," a name that many modern Jews find distressing. ("Lord" has always conjured up the image of lord of the manor to me. And the God-name "King" puts me in the uncomfortable position of praying to an authority figure with the power to chop off my head.) Also, there are the obvious gender issues with these names.

Mystics like to refer to Shekinah, the feminine aspect of God. Many in the Renewal community also pray to God using "Yah," the first two letters of יהוה, which I find quite strong and celebratory. Other terms for God include Ein Sof, Elohim, HaKadosh (the Holy One), HaShem (the Name), Tzadik (Righteous One), Shophet (Judge), Melech (King), and Ro'eh (Shepherd). In the end, Rabbi Prager's siddur invites the worshipper to use the God-name, language, and gender that best reflects his or her own experience of the Divine.

The opening niggun was over. "Shabbat Shalom," Ingber said. He told us how much he looked forward to welcoming and receiving the Sabbath with us. Then he and the musicians launched into "Shalom Aleichem," a song based on a sixteenth century liturgical poem that welcomes the angels who accompany a person home on the eve of the Sabbath, according to a homiletic teaching of the Talmud. When I was growing up, we sang "Shalom Aleichem" full-throated, to an upbeat melody. I liked the softer, haunting, more mysterious melody they sang at Romemu infinitely better.

The service kept tugging at my emotions. Most of the liturgy was in Hebrew and English, but it also included rhythms and inflections from the diaspora languages of Yiddish, Ladino, and also Arabic. I especially liked how "Shabbat" was used interchangeably with "Shabbos"—the Yiddish term my grandmother used. It took me back to the Friday evening dinners and sing-alongs with my aunt Fern.

When I was growing up, very few people in my Conservative synagogue community attended Friday and Saturday morning services unless there was a bar or bat mitzvah or the Sabbath coincided with one of the High Holidays. Even on Rosh Hashanah and Yom Kippur, when the synagogue was packed, it seemed that an unsettling number of the attendees were in a hurry to leave. I could look in any direction and see women going off to the bathroom, and men either dozing or looking at their watches. The atmosphere at Romemu couldn't have been more different. Throughout the service, people got up spontaneously to dance or raise their arms to the sky. There was laughing—and weeping. The meditative silences were long and deep. I sensed that Romemu was the lifeblood of my fellow worshippers, the place where they wanted, more than anywhere else that night, to be.

Near the beginning of the service, Ingber invited us to meditate for a few minutes using any practice or technique we found useful. He hoped that the meditative silence would help us put the worries of the week behind us and attune ourselves to our deeper spiritual needs. For inspiration, he recited a poem by Mary Oliver that reinforced the notion that the day of rest was also a day of soul-work.

We turned to our prayer books. I was happy to see that the Hebrew I had learned as a child hadn't left me. Although I didn't understand what most of the words meant, I could sight-read Hebrew and keep pace with the service. On the few occasions I got lost, I simply hummed along, or let the music take my mind and emotions wherever they wanted to go. As Ingber had said at the beginning of the service, "Words are just one doorway in."

Many of the translations had been done by Reb Zalman Schachter-Shalomi, Renewal's cofounder. There was a romantic and mystical quality to them—"Rush my love, be quick! The time for love is now!"—which conveyed the intensity and intimacy of his relationship with the Divine.

Before saying Judaism's holiest prayer, the Shema, we sang Ahavat Olam, which calls on the presence of love in all creation. "We are loved by an unending love," we sang in English. "Even when we are hidden from ourselves" and "too proud for soothing" and "too embittered to hear." As I sang along, swaying with the rest of the crowd, I sensed that it wasn't simply God that was providing this neverending love; it was the God in each of us, bonded together in this community of strangers, friends, and seekers who were there to embrace, touch, soothe, and counsel each other, through good times and bad. After years of feeling so alienated from Judaism, of feeling so not at home and torn in a million directions when I attended a synagogue, to be in the midst of so much love made me feel like crying.

At the end of the service—after the Amidah and Mourner's Kaddish—Ingber invited everyone who was at Romemu for the first time to stand and introduce themselves. About twenty people stood up, including me. They had come from all over New York, including Brooklyn, Staten Island, Queens, and Westchester County. There were visitors from as far away as Israel and California. A few had grown up in Orthodox households. Others had been raised Reform or Conservative or by parents who had put their energies into leftist politics and healing the world. There was an interfaith couple and two rabbis who were interested in seeing how Romemu did things. Many of these first-time visitors had been scarred by an experience in their birthright religion, and now they wanted to find a spiritual home that was warm, tolerant, respectful of other religions and traditions, and where they could be themselves. They wanted a spiritual home that spoke to the heart and guided them in their everyday lives, where they could feel more joyous and alive.

Because I was standing in the way back, I was one of the last to speak. I said, "I'm Lee Kravitz. I come from a few blocks away—on Riverside Drive, at 110th Street. I'm very happy to be here."

I didn't give any other indication of why I was there. I didn't mention how I had been raised in a Conservative synagogue in Cleveland where the services lacked emotion and joy. Or that I had been married in a suburb of Detroit by the founder of Humanistic Judaism, who believed that God was a figment of the imagination that kept Jews (and believers in other traditions) from taking responsibility for their own lives.

I didn't say what my wife believed: that, if God existed, he wouldn't have allowed her brother Jonny to die such a violent death, and he wouldn't have kept her father from living long enough to play with our children.

Nor did I share any of my own struggles. But if I had, I would have said, *I've been on a long pilgrimage, through a variety of practices and traditions, in search of a spiritual home. This evening it seems that all the roads I've traveled have led me here, to Romemu, just a few blocks away from where I live with my family. It's an amazing feeling— to worship, this Sabbath evening, in the company of fellow seekers. But I feel like I need to test the waters more and see if my excitement about Romemu not only continues, but grows.*

Over the next few weeks, I read up on Rabbi Ingber and watched some interviews with him on YouTube. From what I could glean, he grew up on Long Island in a Modern Orthodox family that observed Jewish law and traditions but also believed in interacting with the non-Jewish, secular world. In high school, he was a competitive bodybuilder. After high school, he spent several years in Israel and then Brooklyn studying at ultra-Orthodox yeshivot that focused on small-group study of the Torah and Talmud, the sacred Jewish texts. Like his ultra-Orthodox peers, he grew his beard and side curls (or payot) long and wore a black top hat and tzitzit, the white fringes twined with blue that observant Jews wear on the corners of their clothing to remind themselves to remember God in their deeds.

But Ingber became so intensely focused on studying Torah and following Jewish law that he became a stranger to himself: "I started feeling dead inside," he recalled. "Much about Judaism still resonated with me—the Sabbath, the songs, the sense of community I felt studying Torah. But I had also ingested the toxicity, the image of God as demanding and punishing, the fact that no matter how much Torah you knew, it wouldn't be enough. You could never be good enough. I needed to get away from that. I needed to heal and become alive again."

At the age of twenty-three, he abandoned Judaism. Over the next ten years, he studied philosophy and psychology at New York University. He explored Buddhism and other sacred wisdom traditions. He took "all sorts of classes" in yoga, shiatsu, kung fu, and tai chi. He taught Pilates and the martial arts. He became a certified astrologer.

To make ends meet, Ingber waited tables at Carmine's, a family-style Italian restaurant on Manhattan's Upper West Side. There was a Jewish study group in the basement of the shul next door, where he'd go during breaks. He had forgotten how much he loved reading and studying Torah. He started thinking about becoming a rabbi.

Shortly after 9/11, Ingber met the man who would change his life and become his rebbe. (The Yiddish word "rebbe," derived from the Hebrew "rabbi," means "master, teacher, and mentor.") Ingber has described his first encounter with Reb Zalman, as he is commonly called, as "love at first sight." Although Reb Zalman was deeply rooted in Jewish tradition, he was also revitalizing it. "He helped me see where a yoga practice could be part of your service to God."

After Reb Zalman ordained him as a Renewal rabbi in 2004, Ingber took a job as rabbi-in-residence at what he calls a "Jewish ashram" in upstate New York. There he started dreaming about beginning his own shul for people who wanted to daven and connect to God with their body, mind, heart, and spirit, as he did. With the support of several New Yorkers and his rebbe's blessing, he began holding services at the shul he called Romemu in 2006. When I attended my first service at Romemu six years later, it had more than three hundred member families. On Friday nights, as many as four hundred people attended services, with more than a thousand people crowding in on Rosh Hashanah and Yom Kippur. For his creative prayer services, *Newsweek* had just listed Ingber as one of America's most influential rabbis.

I was eager to take another class with him. So I signed up for a seminar he was giving at the NYU Center for Spiritual Life in Greenwich Village. The seminar, called "Leaving the Narrow Place," promised to "explore the profound possibilities that Passover offers for gaining insight into the human condition."

For most of my life, I had viewed the holiday of Passover through a strictly historical lens. Passover celebrates the story of how Moses led the Jewish people out of slavery in Egypt. As one of history's great freedom and civil rights stories, it has helped sensitize me to

the oppression of people all over the world—a topic of major concern to me during my thirty-year career as a journalist. Ingber
seemed to have a very different view of Passover. He referred to it
at the beginning of the seminar as "a Buddhist holiday"—a vehicle
for freeing oneself from the suffering caused by our compulsions
and distorted thinking.

At the start of the seminar, Ingber asked us to introduce ourselves.
There were about ten of us—a diverse group: One woman worked
on an organic farm, another was a relationship expert who had appeared on TV; there were a couple of men who seemed excited
about delving deeper into the mystical aspects of the Torah; and a
woman who said she was an architect who designed sacred public
spaces. Two people—a younger woman and a middle-aged man—
were avid meditators; in fact, they each had led meditation sessions
before Saturday morning services at Romemu. It was a group of
interesting, articulate people who had come from a variety of Jewish
backgrounds and knew Hebrew to varying degrees. When it was my
turn, I described myself as being on a midlife pilgrimage through
different spiritual traditions and practices. "I've been yearning for
God and a spiritual home," I said. It was clear that I hadn't been
alone in that longing.

After a short meditation, Ingber said that "Pesach is all about
orality: eating, speaking, silence, and prayer." He noted a sixteenth
century kabbalist's observation that "Pesach" means "mouth talks"
or "the mouth that speaks" in Hebrew. Moses, the protagonist of the
Passover story, has trouble speaking: He tells God that he is "slow of
speech and tongue" (Exodus 4:10). He's afraid that Pharaoh will
never listen to him, "since I speak with faltering lips" (Exodus 6:12).

As slaves, the Jews are similarly limited. "'Egypt' ('Mitzrayim' in Hebrew) means 'a place of narrowing' in Hebrew, where you have no access to language and hence no identity," Ingber explained. Because he has difficulty speaking, Moses is able to empathize with the Israelites and give language to that which can't be expressed. "Moses is the wounded healer."

For most of my life I had viewed Moses as a larger-than-life storybook hero. But now I was seeing him through a different lens, as a man full of doubts and insecurities. I remembered how I had exiled myself to the back of my class in elementary school, and never left that narrowing place, not even in college, because I was afraid that if I spoke people would laugh at my speech impediments (I had a lisp and pronounced *r*'s as if they were *w*'s) or realize that I had nothing of value to say. So I literally kept my distance. And because I went to such great lengths not to talk, I didn't get any better at speaking in public. Instead, I disappeared deeper and deeper into myself and became weak and voiceless, as the Israelites had been in Egypt.

Passover revolves around the seder, the structured retelling of the Exodus story. "The Jews gave narrative to the world—the notion that there is a beginning, middle, and end to stories, a narrative arc," Ingber said. "That's what we bequeathed to Western civilization: storytelling. And the ability to find words and concepts to release us from our suffering. Passover is the original talking cure."

The idea that Passover could be a vehicle for self-awareness and spiritual growth was a revelation to me. Paraphrasing the Baal Shem Tov, the founder of Hasidism, Ingber said that we should use the Passover story to "gain clarity" in our lives. One of the highlights of the seder for me has always been when the youngest child present recites the "Four Questions," a way of explaining some of the rituals that make Passover different from other nights. Ingber proposed that the seder should also feature questions for the soul. For example: "Did anyone at this seder overcome a major obstacle in their spiritual life during the past year? If so, tell us about it." Or: "How can you tell your own story in a way that releases you from suffering rather than enslaves you further?" I loved his idea: a seder for seekers.

A week later, on my way to the second Passover class, I stopped to get a slice of spinach and mozzarella pizza. Before I took the first bite, I felt hungry (as usual) for more, so I ordered a slice of sausage and mushroom. As a result, instead of enjoying just one slice, I ended up feeling both guilty and out of control for wolfing down two. Then, at the bodega next door, I bought an energy drink that contained the caffeine equivalent of two cups of coffee and four hundred milligrams of niacin. This guaranteed that, during the opening meditation, I'd be plagued by a growling stomach (from the pizza) and a racing heart. And since the theme of the seminar was orality, I had a heightened awareness of one of my biggest problems: my compulsion (since childhood) to eat everything on my plate and more, even when I was full, out of a fear that I'd be hungry later. When I was younger and more active, my overeating didn't seem to be an issue—in fact, it endeared me to my mother and grandmothers, because I was the one child who seemed to eat and enjoy everything they cooked. But as I got older and my metabolism changed, my compulsive eating had become an issue for me: I kept gaining weight and belly fat, which contributed to my blood pressure and cholesterol problems and my sluggishness. My doctors had told me to reduce the calories I took in and lose ten or, better yet, twenty pounds. But I couldn't. I felt compelled to keep eating.

The second class focused on the significance of eating only un-leavened bread, called matzah, on Passover. Since the Israelites left Egypt hastily, they did not have time for the bread to rise, so it was made without yeast. Jewish law doesn't just mandate the eating of matzah, the "bread of affliction," during Passover. It prohibits Jews from owning, eating, or benefiting from leavened bread, or hametz, during the holiday.

Technically, hametz is any product made from one of five types of grain—typically wheat, barley, rye, spelt, or oats—and yeast. Combined with water and flour, it needs to stand for longer than 18 minutes so that the yeast can rise.

Matzah, on the other hand, is made in 18 minutes or less. To Jewish mystics, the number 18 is intrinsic to the greater meaning of matzah, according to Ingber. Hametz begins with a "chet," the eighth letter of the Hebrew alphabet. The word "chai" is spelled with a chet and a yud, which has a value of 10—together they equal 18. So 18 equals chai, that is, "to be alive." "In the Hasidic tradi-tion, hametz is an expression of egoic fullness—of being puffed up, of being full of oneself," Ingber said. Matzah, on the other hand, is only baked to the bare minimum of what it takes "to be alive" and goes no further. "In other words," Ingber said, "matzah is un-adorned ego."

He started to riff. "Hametz is matzah on steroids, or matzah on a big ego trip. It's the way we inflate our personal stories in order to hide our deep wounds and real selves." He compared hametz to avidyā, the Buddhist concept for "the opposite of knowledge." "Hametz is anything we add to our stories that obscures the true nature of things. Matzah is the truly nourishing place of nothing added and just what you need."

Throughout the session, many of my fellow attendees offered

memories of the hametz-cleaning rituals in their own families. For example, their grandparents would fill small plastic bags with the hametz they swept up from around the house, and give away the bread, pastries, and other baked goods that were still usable to non-Jewish friends and local charities. I had no such memories. In my parents' household, while we ate matzah at the Passover seder, the hametz stayed hidden in the kitchen cabinets. My mother wasn't in the habit of throwing anything out, and she liked eating her bologna and cheese sandwiches exclusively on white bread. If my grandparents had a hametz-cleaning ritual, I was never aware of it.

And I certainly wasn't aware of any deeper mystical meaning to the bread of affliction. "In Kabbalah there's a quality called malchut—the radical receptive principle," Ingber said. "To be receptive like the moon is to be a great value: You have no light of your own, you receive light; you're an empty vessel, you're receiving God's grace. That's the mind of the righteous person, the bodhisattva, the tzadik, the enlightened being: Christ mind, the mind that receives the object without adding all the embellishments."

The great Jewish mystics put Moses in that category, according to Ingber. "Moses was a clear vessel, a clear mirror, because he received God's light without adding all of his own stories to it, he was able to receive the Divine without all the embellishments. And so to be like Moses is to be matzah-esque, to be matzah-like. Matzah means I have no ambitions to be a big loaf of bread. Or a challah, bagel, or croissant." Or a second slice of pizza, I thought to myself.

As Reb Zalman had taught him, Ingber liked to think of Passover as an opportunity to clear away "the metaphorical hametz hiding our hearts," to get rid of everything in our past that is no longer alive or essential for us. He suggested two more questions for the soul: "What must I let go of to feel connected to my simplicity?"

Then, paraphrasing Eric Berne, the author of *Games People Play*, he asked, "What are my trips?"

He listed some of his own: "My rabbi trip, my holier-than-thou trip, my I-know-so-much-Bible trip. The trips that keep me from being present for the people I love."

I liked the fact that this charismatic young rabbi was alert to his vulnerabilities as he built his shul and a following. Perhaps that would make him less susceptible to becoming a guru of the sort I hated. Like all of us, rabbis are human. They get tempted by power and other people's expectations of them. They are also fragile, which was why I liked the way Ingber ended his discussion of matzah with the observation that "matzah also represents brokenness," as in Humpty Dumpty falling off the wall, or the tablets breaking into pieces when Moses threw them down in anger from Mount Sinai.

At the beginning of the seder, the head of the household breaks a piece of matzah in half. Then he wraps one of the halves (called the "afikoman") in a napkin and hides it. Toward the end of the meal, he invites the children to look for the afikoman. The child who finds it gets a piece of candy or a small amount of money. Then the afikoman is reunited with the other half of matzah and eaten as part of dessert. The much-anticipated hunt for the afikoman was perhaps the only thing that kept me and my brothers awake during the long seders of our childhood. But Ingber noted the afikoman's deeper, mystical meaning: "You have to break the matzah for it to reveal its secrets. Our hearts are the same way. By putting the matzah and our hearts together again, we make ourselves whole."

All that talk of leavened and unleavened bread was making me hungry again—for more pizza. Maybe a couple slices of mushroom and onion or eggplant with extra cheese. I could eat them on the way to the subway. But thankfully, Rabbi Ingber's final riff—on

"Dayenu," one of Passover's most popular songs—helped put the kibosh on my gluttonous plans.

"Dayenu" means "it would have been enough for us" in Hebrew. The song has fifteen stanzas. Each one expresses gratitude to God— for bringing us out of Egypt, for giving us the Sabbath and Torah, for taking us to the Land of Israel, and so forth. After each stanza, everyone at the table exuberantly sings "Dayenu" several times, conveying that it would have been enough for God to have done just one of these things, but he did them all, bestowing a bounty of blessings on the Jews.

"Is anything ever enough?" Ingber asked. "Can we ever be truly sated?" That was the question "Dayenu" posed to each of us as members of a consumerist society. "How much do I really need—in square feet of house, in speed of car, in adoration from friends and family, in praise for my accomplishments, in salary, in bling—to feel as free as the Jews did when they left Egypt? Each of us needs to ask ourselves those questions, because, as the Buddhists say, if there isn't an enough, we may be doomed to endless suffering."

I walked out of class and down the street singing, "Da-da-yenu," to myself. Past the bodega and pizza shop, down the stairs into the subway. When I got home, I told Elizabeth about the distinction Ingber had made between matzah and hametz, and about his interpretation of "Dayenu." Surprisingly, she was interested in what I was saying. When I told her that I had come to the conclusion that I was spreading myself too thin, she said, "Maybe it's time to clear away the hametz." I laughed. I told her that I wanted to keep her and the kids, of course, but there were other relationships and activities that felt stale to me, or like they were no longer essential. Especially if I were to devote more time to going to synagogue, studying Torah, or participating in activities that might bind me to a particular spiritual community.

For example, the nonprofit boards I served on had clearly become hametz. Not because I didn't think the activities were important—they were. But I could no longer help these organizations as much as I could when I was a magazine editor, with connections and editorial pages to leverage on their behalf. Similarly, I loved being a baseball coach—for Ben and Noah but also for other young people. But now that my boys were older and playing in more competitive leagues, they needed coaches who knew a lot more than I did. It was time for me to clear away the hametz of coaching, although I'd still be in the stands with Elizabeth for the truly matzah-esque pleasure of cheering on our kids.

Gathering

April Through September

At the beginning of my quest for a spiritual home, I had made a pledge not to venture abroad or to distant places to find God— but to stay within two hours of my family and our apartment on 110th Street and Riverside Drive. The one exception was when we traveled as a family to Barcelona, Spain, during the kids' spring vacation, which coincided with Passover and Easter. Because my family was with me, I felt justified in exploring places in the Catalan region of Spain that might inspire me or give me spiritual perspective.

To make the trip affordable, we swapped apartments for the week with a family that lived in the center of Barcelona, near the major sights and museums and within walking distance of the Plaça d'Espanya train station, the hub for day trips into Catalonia. I was particularly excited about visiting two places—Sagrada Família, one of the most famous cathedrals in the world, which was in Barcelona, and Montserrat, a mountain to the northwest of the city, and which was home to a well-known boys' choir, a community of Benedictine monks, and a statue of the Black Madonna that drew thousands of visitors and pilgrims each year.

From Plaça d'Espanya, it took a little more than an hour for us to reach the foot of Montserrat by train; then we took a funicular railway, a cable car of sorts, up to the top. "Montserrat" means "serrated or jagged mountain." Thousands of years of erosion, climate change, and movements in the earth's crust have carved dramatic cliffs, caves, and crevices into the limestone, so that the multipeaked mountain looks otherworldly—and ripe for supernatural visions and miracles.

On the way up we could see abandoned caves in the cliffs, where reclusive monks once lived. And then we reached the top, with its view of the Pyrenees and green valley below.

Of the various paths leading up and down the mountain, it was the 2.7-kilometer walk to Santa Cova, site of Montserrat's most famous miracle, that I wanted to take the most.

Legend has it that in 880 C.E., near dusk on a Saturday evening, a group of shepherd children heard a beautiful song and witnessed a great light falling from the sky. Five Saturdays later, after similar visions, elders from the village found the image of the Virgin Mary on the walls of a nearby cave. Soon thereafter, there were more miracles. A group of Benedictine monks built a monastery on Montserrat in 1025 C.E. Then, in the late twelfth century, a carving was made of the image of the Holy Mother, followed by more alleged miracles. Ignatius of Loyola (in the fifteenth century) and Pope John Paul II (in the twentieth) were among the thousands of pilgrims who have come to pray at the site; so were Cervantes, who wrote *Don Quixote*, and Columbus, who named an island in the Caribbean after Montserrat. Because of its rich history, the Catalan people consider

Montserrat the spiritual heart of their effort to achieve independence from Spain.

I wanted to go to Santa Cova, which was just over an hour's walk from the monastery, because I felt that it would set the stage visually and narratively for me to understand the mountain's unique power as a place of pilgrimage. What I didn't count on were the many detours that would keep me from ever getting there. Every few steps Caroline would see a grouping of wildflowers she wanted to photograph. Or there'd be a rock jutting out over the valley, and she'd pose her brothers on it. Elizabeth was going from rock to rock doing yoga poses. Twenty minutes into the walk we had only gotten a few hundred feet and the boys and Caroline, having captured enough images to share with their friends on Facebook, were getting thirsty and antsy, as was Elizabeth. After weighing the options, I decided that the chances of my losing them for the rest of the afternoon were so great that it was imperative for me to follow them back to town.

We had soft drinks in the shade, then walked toward the Gothic basilica that was adjacent to the Santa Maria de Montserrat Abbey. The monastery was closed to the public, but you could stand in line to tour the basilica and pay homage to the Black Madonna in the back of the church. Along the way, I pointed out various biblical scenes and references to the kids: the statue of Saint Benedict, founder of the Catholic religious order that bears his name; the pillars dedicated to the prophets Ezekiel, Jeremiah, Isaiah, and Daniel; the small chapels devoted to scenes from the lives of Jesus and Mary. Soon enough, we were face-to-face with the icon that has drawn so many pilgrims to Montserrat over the last eight hundred years: La Moreneta ("The little dark-skinned one" in Catalan), the best-known Black Madonna statue in Spain.

The wooden carving sits on an ornate silver throne that was

given to the basilica by the Catalan people in 1947 to mark the end of the Spanish Civil War. Sitting upright on Mary's lap, the Christ child wears a crown. In her right hand, Mary holds a round bowl that represents his power over all the universe.

Mary's round face has open and expressive eyes and a Mona Lisa smile. Close up, I could see the black paint darkening the brown poplar; the paint on her left hand is worn away because of pilgrims kissing it. I didn't feel anything special in the presence of La Moreneta. But using my imagination a little, I could picture what pilgrims from all over the world must feel like when they stand before her, their lives filled with pain, heartbreak, and worries. In Luke 1:48, Mary is quoted as saying of God and herself, "For he hath regarded the low estate of his handmaiden: for behold, from henceforth all generations will call me blessed." Standing before the Black Madonna, believers who make the pilgrimage must feel a profound sense of hope and relief, for this transfigured handmaiden is proof that God will pour blessings on them and their loved ones, too.

After we left the basilica, it was time to take a cable car down the mountain and catch the train back to Barcelona. During the ride, Elizabeth read a novel and the kids made small talk with some other children their age, including an Irish boy who was spending the year in Barcelona with his aunt. Meanwhile, I read a small book about Montserrat's community of Benedictine monks.

The restrictions I had placed on my spiritual search had kept me from spending time in a monastery, but as I looked for a spiritual home at Romemu and elsewhere, I was aware that men and women had been bonding together in religious communities since the time of Jesus. While researching my first book I spent several days in a Greek Orthodox monastery in Etna, California, which had been founded by a childhood friend of mine who had been a monk since college. My goal in visiting my friend was to see how my life might have turned out if I had followed his path instead of my own. There were many aspects of his monastic life that appealed to me: the rhythm of the day, marked by prayer services, work, meals, and periods of silence that kept God front of mind; the emphasis on humility; the closeness the monks felt to each other and to God.

At night, as snow fell, the monastery seemed to be a world unto itself: timeless, mystical, the quiet broken only by the sounds of hymns and prayers. I liked that. But I didn't like the idea of not having Elizabeth and the kids in my life, or the level of obedience the monastic life demanded. The archbishop there was brilliant, wise, and funny, and I could have learned a great deal from him. But I could never see being so obedient to the dictates of another human being.

As I read about the hundred Benedictine monks who lived on Montserrat, I had a similar reaction. I loved the rhythm of their prayerful life and their sense of community. I also liked how the order had maintained the monastery and their faith against tremendous odds. (After twenty-three monks had been killed there during the Spanish Civil War, the ones who survived rebuilt the basilica so that it could remain a place of pilgrimage.) However, the idea of surrendering so many freedoms to an abbot who had the power to determine what I read and how I spent my time, who had the power to punish and even banish me, rubbed against my most essential grain.

The second stop on my vacation pilgrimage was the Basilica of Sagrada Famíla in Barcelona. When he began working on Sagrada Família in 1883, twenty-nine-year-old architect Antoni Gaudí was already famous for his innovative use of color, material, and form. The cathedral became Gaudí's life's work until he died in 1927. It remains a work in progress, one of the most audacious, ambitious, and imaginative examples of sacred architecture in the world.

The entrance fee to Sagrada Família is steep, so Elizabeth and I decided that she and the kids would walk around La Rambla, the main shopping area of Barcelona, while I toured the cathedral. I could have spent days there. Gaudí is known for his imagination, but I wasn't prepared for how deeply his creativity, in devotion to God and his Roman Catholic faith, would affect me.

On the outside, carved frogs, dragons, lizards, and salamanders cling to the cathedral, warding off rainwater. The pinnacles are capped with grasses and ears of wheat. Inside and out, plants and animals seem to emerge organically from the stone, heralding both the savior and the arrival of a regenerated world.

I went from scene to amazing scene: the Coronation of Mary, the Slaughter of Innocents, the Betrothal of the Virgin and Saint Mary, all sculpted into the stone. Jesus prays sorrowfully at Gethsemane; the soldiers play dice for his robe; the centurion lances Jesus in the side. I had seen dozens of paintings in museums and books of these biblical moments, but none had brought me to the verge of tears as now.

Standing in the center of the basilica, I was aware, more than anything, of the quality of light. Gaudí had wanted the basilica to be supported by a system of columns that imitated the form and structure of a tree, so that the sun's rays, shining down from the cupola, give you the impression of being alone with God in the forest.

Standing there, bathed in this remarkable celestial light, I imagined Gaudí working day and night in his studio, transforming the stone—but also himself, into a more spiritual being. His biographers have written that, when he began the project, he wore elegant clothes and spent his evenings with Barcelona's other movers and shakers. But as Sagrada Família began taking shape, he moved into a lonely studio on the premises, where his faith deepened and he became more and more of an ascetic. By the time of the accident that killed him—he was struck by a tram after having wandered into the street—he was so disheveled from absorption in his project that bystanders mistook him for a homeless man. And yet, as I stood in his remarkable cathedral, thinking about his art and his death, I was grateful that he had persevered.

Such beauty, such devotion, such risk taken to satisfy the deeply human yearning for God—these were evident at Montserrat and at Sagrada Família, where individually and as a community the faithful pray. In these places I was moved to feel gratitude and awe, just as I was in the unadorned Quaker Meeting room in Riverside Church, the kirtan-filled lecture hall at Omega, and the church at the corner of 105th Street and Amsterdam Avenue where I had started davening with other seekers and Jews.

As for my children, their big spiritual experience in Barcelona didn't happen in a church, synagogue, or on the top of a jagged mountain. It occurred in a sports stadium on the Tuesday before Easter Sunday. Shopping for God as I was, I saw everything I did and encountered through a spiritual lens. Walking from the apartment to the stadium with hundreds and then thousands of other people, it struck me that we were truly on a pilgrimage—to Camp Nou, home of FC Barcelona, the most valuable sports franchise in the world.

FC Barcelona is more than a soccer team or sports club—it is the wellspring of Catalan identity, pride, and nationalism. En route to the stadium, the pilgrims chanted, "Barça, Barça, Barça." Celebrants of every age and gender wore blue and claret jerseys that paid homage to their team and favorite players. At the start of the game, they rose to chant "El Cant del Barça," the team's theme song, swaying back and forth in unison, sharing vibrations and heart rhythms with the rest of their fellow Catalonians.

Ben and Noah were in sports-fan heaven. Elizabeth rooted for FC Barcelona with a zeal she usually reserves for teams from Detroit. And like everyone else in the crowd, we went crazy whenever Lionel "Leo" Messi, the world's greatest soccer player, had the ball. Messi, with his quick feet and matchless timing. Messi, with his humble, joyous demeanor. Messi, who weaves through the rival teams of other cities and countries like a whirling dervish to make miraculous kicks and game-winning goals.

He did it this night, too. Wearing the sacred number 10 on his jersey, he scored the winning goal. Messi the Messiah, Messi the Savior. Messi who had just given me and my family an evening of almost spiritual bliss.

Now that I had become so interested in Jewish Renewal, it was time to do what Faith Linda had advised and meet the movement's founder—Rabbi Zalman Schachter-Shalomi. He was scheduled to make a rare trip east from Boulder, Colorado, where he lived, to the Isabella Freedman Jewish Retreat Center in Connecticut, where about two hundred people would be gathering at the end of May for a five-day celebration of Shavuot, one of Judaism's three major pilgrim festivals.

Reb Zalman was born in Poland and raised in Vienna. Fleeing the Nazis, he came to the United States in 1941 at the age of seventeen. In 1947, after several years of study, he was ordained as an Orthodox rabbi within the Chabad-Lubavitch community of Hasidic Jews.

In the early 1950s, Menachem Mendel Schneerson, the head of the Chabad-Lubavitch movement, sent Reb Zalman and another promising young rabbi named Shlomo Carlebach to the West Coast to bring an alienated and materialistic generation of Jews back to Judaism. (Carlebach, known as the "Singing Rabbi," ended up composing hundreds of uplifting and ecstatic songs that are now sung in synagogues throughout the world.) In the process, Reb Zalman came into contact with some of the major countercultural figures and ideas of the 1960s, and experimented with what he called "the sacramental value of lysergic acid," or LSD. He left the Lubavitch movement and embarked on a period of spiritual risk-taking and innovation that led him to promote interfaith dialogue, feminism, LBGT membership, and new approaches to Jewish law. He also championed many of the prayer innovations that I'd experienced at Romemu, including meditation, chanting, and spontaneous movement and dance.

I had expected the eighty-nine-year-old rabbi to be frail and listless. Instead, he was a font of energy and wisdom. In his gray vest, black fedora, and round eyeglasses, he had a certain Old World elegance, punctuated by a wispy gray beard and his huge, easy smile. Also, he clearly understood his role that weekend: to be the chief davener and nourish the community he had helped spawn with fresh spiritual insights.

Shavuot, the occasion for this gathering, follows Passover by fifty days. It originally marked the end of the seven weeks of the barley harvest and the beginning of the wheat harvest. Indeed, before the First Temple in Jerusalem was destroyed in 586 BCE, Jewish men were expected to bring their first omer, or sheaf, of barley to the temple as a thanksgiving offering.

Shavuot also celebrates Moses' return from the top of Mount

Sinai with the two stone tablets that contained the Ten Command-ments, the fundamental laws of the Jewish faith. On Passover, Jews recall how God freed the Israelites from slavery in Egypt. Shavuot commemorates the next big event, when God gave the Jewish peo-ple the Torah and they committed themselves, as a nation, to serv-ing him.

Over the next few days I participated in prayer services, nature walks, an all-night vigil, Torah Yoga, candle lightings, Torah read-ings, and seminars by many of the leading figures in Jewish Re-newal, including Rabbi Ingber, Rabbi Arthur Waskow, Rabbi Phyllis Berman, and Rabbi Marcia Prager. There was a good deal of debate about the meaning of the terrifying events at Sinai: the smoke and fire, the shaking of the earth, the voice that boomed out, "Anochi HaShem Elokecha"—"I am the Name, your God." And there was even more about the meaning of what had happened next at the foot of the mountain: the forging of a spiritual community and group identity based on service to God.

During one session a woman asked, "If there was Anochi, or undifferentiated holiness, at the beginning, why did God let duality happen?" It was the same question Shyamdas had grappled with when he pondered the difference between saguna and nirguna.

Reb Zalman answered by saying, "Because there was a need to love in the undifferentiated holiness. And to love you need an object to love." It was a stunning way to convey the importance of seeing God and God's love in everyone and in nature, too.

I had come to this retreat to see Reb Zalman in action. But I had also come to get a fuller sense of the community of people who had found a spiritual home and identity in Jewish Renewal. As at Romemu, they were a varied group that seemed to share a few basic principles: that prayer should be enlivening; that everyone should have an equal opportunity to worship, no matter their race, gender, or sexual orientation; that seeking and trying on new ideas and practices is a natural and necessary part of spiritual growth; that healing the hurts and hatreds within each of us is a prelude to healing and improving the world.

I shared those principles and, although I wasn't gifted in metaphysical thought (in fact, too much speculation of that sort exhausted me), I did enjoy hearing Renewal's rabbis puzzle through the paradoxes and ponder what it meant to get closer to God.

My one qualm was the degree of charismatic leadership in the movement. As egalitarian and progressive as Jewish Renewal was, it seemed that all eyes were on Reb Zalman—and that one day they would be on Rabbi Ingber, his most likely successor. Did the guru worship that rubbed so harshly against my grain play a major role in this community I was thinking of joining?

I raised that question throughout the weekend in conversations with many attendees, including a woman who knew the dark side of gurus better, perhaps, than any person on earth. In the 1970s Anna Rayne-Levi, a therapist now living in Santa Fe, New Mexico, had been head of security for Rajneesh, the Indian guru who was later known as Osho. (The organization had two main ashrams—one in Pune, India, the other in a small town in Oregon.) After years of witnessing his drug-taking and indifference to child and sexual abuse among his aides, she helped bring about a federal investigation of the cult.

When I told her of my qualms about charismatic leadership in Jewish Renewal, Rayne-Levi told me, "There's some of it. But it's nothing—and I mean nothing—like what was going on among the Rajneeshis. In the ashrams in Pune and Oregon, the ecstatic singing and dancing was manipulative, and Rajneesh used free love and drugs to cement his control. Reb Zalman has been my teacher for more than thirty years, and he is beyond reproach."

Earlier that day I had been chatting with Anna's fifteen-year-old son Rayne, who struck me as being one of the most spiritually engaged young people I'd ever met. When I told her that, she said, "He's been asking the 'big questions' about life, existence, and God since he was in diapers."

Rayne was wearing a yarmulke and tzitzit at the retreat. But when I asked him about them, he told me that it was unusual for him to wear them in public. The one time he had worn them to school, he was mocked so badly that he decided he'd never do it again. I was old enough to be Rayne's father, or even grandfather, but I felt like I was talking to a soul mate. He had meditated with Buddhists and chanted with Hindus, and he was asking himself many of the same questions I had been asking myself about God and prayer.

I asked him what he wanted to do with everything he was learning. He said, "I want to make spirituality relevant, cool, and understandable for young people." An ambitious and praiseworthy goal. But I wondered how my own kids would have responded to this unusually serious and self-possessed young man. Generally, they were suspicious of kids who gravitated so easily to adults, or who wore their religion on their sleeve. Would they have dismissed Rayne at a glance, or given him a chance? For the past two years, Ben and Caroline had seemed indifferent to my own quest—they treated it as "Daddy's thing," not their own, and sought very few details about what I was either doing or feeling. And Noah rolled his eyes whenever I invited him to accompany me to a kirtan concert or service at Romemu. I couldn't hold the fact that my children weren't as spiritually motivated as Rayne or me against them. For, in truth, they were doing the hard teenage work of building relationships and self-confidence while they spent their weekends hanging out with friends.

So much had changed since the days when my great-grandfather Chatza went to shul in Lithuania. Reb Zalman was far more progressive and worldly than anyone Chatza had known, and his openhearted take on Judaism—informed, as it was, by his knowledge of Sufism, transpersonal psychology, and Buddhism—would have struck my peasant ancestors as strange. But I think they would have easily recognized the piety in the rebbe's davening, and shared a shot of schnapps with him at the end of the Sabbath service, because there was something simple, joyous, and intimate in the way he prayed.

"O God, our parents' God, take pleasure in the way we do Shabbos and sing the Avoteinu," he prayed. "Make us satisfied. Feed us well. In the places where we're despairing, make us happy. Make true our hearts so we really do the Shabbos service in truth, in right motive, and the right energy. And we ask you, give us many more wonderful Shabbatot like this one." When he said this last line, I detected a tremor in his voice—perhaps an acknowledgment of his own mortality and a desire that the spirit of this davening would go on after he passed away.

More than anything else, this Renewal community I was thinking of joining was a community united in prayer. Rabbi Ingber called Reb Zalman the "prayer whisperer"—and, during a question-and-answer session later in the day, it was clear why. In his opening statement, Reb Zalman informed us that it was the biblical King David's yahrzeit, the anniversary of his death, that day. "The Book of Psalms is a very important thing for us to know," he added of the book ascribed to David. "If somebody says I don't know whether

God listens to my prayers, read through the Book of Psalms. Hear it from someone, David, who was intimate enough with God to say, 'O God, you have searched me and known me. You know when I get up and sit down, you know all my ways, before a thought even comes to me, you know it already.' Then say, as King David did in the Psalms, 'Listen to me, God. Please be my helper.'"

A young man stood up. Earlier that day, I had seen this same man talking to a tree, which apparently wasn't uncommon on Shavuot. "Why, if I'm part of nature, why would I put something like the Psalms in front of me, between me and nature, when I want to pray?" he asked.

Reb Zalman answered him with a question: "Why is it when people are in love that they sing a song that somebody else has written? Because it's there," he said. Then he began humming a song. "Schubert wanted to tell somebody that he loved her. So he wrote this song. It's there to help you. That's all I want to say."

When a man asked Reb Zalman about the future of Jewish Renewal, he said, "All I know is as long as people daven like we davened here on Friday night and this morning, I will be very happy." He said that the continuity of the Jewish people would also depend on the strength of their davening. He was referring to the fact that many Jewish leaders are afraid that the rising number of interfaith and same-sex marriages will result in fewer Jewish families. "The American Jewish Committee and all these groups have committees on continuity, but I am much more interested in davenology," Reb Zalman said. "If people are davening and doing certain types of mitzvoth, there will be continuity. When parents and children can have really good conversations with each other, there will be continuity."

I loved that answer, because it validated how Elizabeth and I were trying to parent our kids—not by commanding them (except when it came to the chores they never seemed to do) but by having good and open conversations with them.

Rayne, who was sitting in the front row, got up next and asked a question that had also been on my own mind. "I'm so deeply rooted in my Judaism," he said. "However, I'm also interested in other spiritual and religious traditions. What would you say to me or to anyone else who is confused about how to include their Judaism in their practices of other religions?"

Reb Zalman began singing the refrain from "Eleanor Rigby," the Beatles' lament to lonely people everywhere. The audience joined in. Then he said, "I want to say that anyone who isn't hyphenated today I'm worried about." By hyphenated, he meant Irish-Mexican, Polish-Russian, Buddhist-Jewish—any one of the thousands of mixed identities that reflect our increasingly global relationships and world. "All of us need a little transplant if we're to be whole. Somebody might need a transplant from Buddhism, or Sufism, or kirtan. As for me, when I'm curious about another tradition, I always go with my kippah [the head covering also known as a yarmulke, worn by observant Jews]. I go to church with my kippah, to peyote meetings with my kippah. A woman once objected that I was wearing a kippah at a Christian meeting. When I was asked to explain why I was wearing it, I said, 'When I'm in the presence of the living God, that's what I always wear.' The elder of the church told me to keep wearing it. 'It's your head,' he said. What a wonderful moment."

He encouraged Rayne to keep exploring other traditions and practices, and to not be afraid of doubt. "Faith without doubt causes a lot of barnacles," he said. "Barnacles of superstition. Doubt is the way that faith manages to keep clean."

At the end of the Q&A session, he told us that he had one more thing he wanted to emphasize about davening. "Whenever you pray to God, look into your heart and ask yourself what blessings do you need that will make your life and feelings so happy that you'll say, 'Baruch HaShem. I thank you, dear God, for making a universe."

On the last day of the retreat, I attended a session called "Gathering 'Round the Mountain," led by Rabbis Arthur Waskow and Phyllis Berman. The mountain in question, of course, was Sinai, where God gave the Jews the Torah and where the Jewish people committed themselves to God and became a community united by faith.

"We've heard the word 'revelation' a lot over the past few days," Berman said. "Revelation as we were taught is not something that happens once; it's a continuous process." She asked us to think about a revelation that had come to us during the retreat. Was it during one of Reb Zalman's teachings? In the chaos of the dining hall? In a chance encounter with a soul mate we'd never met before? And how had that revelation helped us to realign ourselves spiritually? "The gift for each of us," she said, "is to come to each day open to the possibility that revelation is going to happen."

We broke into groups of three, and during the next fifteen minutes Berman urged us to tell our fellow group members the personal journey we had taken to our modern-day Sinai. What had been our Jewish identity growing up? What experiences had made us question our faith, become more spiritually aware, set us off on the path to God? She also asked us to envision the next steps in our journeys.

"Although each story is unique," Berman said, "our stories aren't merely personal. Together, they unfold details of a larger drama: our passionate Jewish quest to approach the Mystery we name God and respond collectively and individually to the manifestations of the Divine. So, too, our stories reflect an even broader tale of the human quest to learn ultimate meaning and live in the light of that knowledge."

She urged us to keep the stories we were told by other people confidential. When the fifteen minutes were up, Waskow told us about a revelation that had come to him the first time he visited the Vietnam Veterans Memorial in Washington, D.C. Standing before the wall, he said, "I realized that the fifty thousand names on the wall were part of one great name—HaShem, the Name that contains the names of every galaxy and every quark, every rock and every mountain, every sentient being."

He shared an apocryphal story with us about two rabbis who were discussing the nature of God's image. One of the rabbis made a distinction Waskow liked: "When Caesar puts his image on a coin, all the coins turn out identical," the rabbi said. "When the Holy One puts his divine image on a coin, all the coins come out unique."

He asked us to stand quietly and look around the room, going from face to unique face. "At each face," he said, "pause for a few seconds and say to yourself, This is the face of God." I did. I looked around the room, and, pausing at each face, I told myself, This is the face of God. As I went from face to face, I could feel my whole body beginning to relax. I was calm, receptive, smiling—just as I had been on the God walks I took before the journey that brought me to this Sinai had started in earnest.

Rabbi Waskow ended the gathering by lifting his eyes to the God who had given the Jewish people the Torah: "You," he prayed, "who are the inter-breathing of all life and every Anochi, who breathe us and whom we breathe, we bless you for making it clear to us, for giving us the awareness, that by breathing together we make a holy connection, that by shaping our breath into words and breathing our words into your sacred Torah, we affirm and renew every Anochi in your hour and earth." Waskow said a final blessing in Hebrew; we answered with a resounding "amen."

After the Shavuot retreat I started attending Romemu on Friday nights, and on Saturdays when I could, too. Each time I sat in a different part of the synagogue, so that I could see and experience different members and their families and imagine whether I'd feel comfortable becoming part of their community. One Saturday morning I went to the 8:30 A.M. yoga class and the 9:30 A.M. meditation group that preceded the 10:00 A.M. Torah service. I liked how much the yoga and meditation focused and energized me for the prayers and chanting.

One Friday evening, after the regular Kabbalah Shabbat service, I had refreshments in the basement of the church with some other prospective members, including a few Columbia students and professors and a young woman who had started her own dance company. I was overjoyed to see such intellectually engaged and talented young people thinking as seriously as I was about joining Romemu, but I also felt sad because Elizabeth wasn't standing there next to me. At times I was aware of feeling like a fish out of water. Was that because I was a married man in a sea of singles and that my theological differences with my wife had forced me to swim these waters alone? Or was it simply that I had never been a joiner?

There were certain people who jumped up and danced spontaneously during the service. And others who joined the "conga line" of worshippers who walked behind Rabbi Ingber as he carried the Torah joyously through the aisles. That wasn't my style. But I sang my heart out during the services, especially as I got to know the melodies better. And almost every time I went to Romemu, there was at least one moment that reminded me of why I had yearned so long for a spiritual home.

Before the recitation of the Mourner's Kaddish, Rabbi Ingber invites anyone who has lost a loved one recently, or who is observing the anniversary of a loved one's death, to stand if they'd like. Then he goes around the room, giving each mourner a chance to say the name of the loved one who has died. The week my Uncle Pudge died, at the age of seventy-seven, I stood along with the other mourners, and when it was my turn, I said, "My uncle: Jack 'Pudgie' Kravitz." I was trembling as I said my uncle's name, but to acknowledge his death supported by a whole congregation of people who had suffered losses in their own lives was both incredibly moving and cathartic. I was probably the only person in the world that night saying Kaddish for my uncle, and it comforted me to do so for him. At the same time, it connected me to the generations of my ancestors who had said Kaddish for their own relatives, and the triumphs and struggles that had been their lives.

I stood up again on the anniversary of my Aunt Fern's death, and then when a friend who had been my protégé took his own life. Besides alleviating my own pain, I felt, in each of these cases, that I was keeping the memory of someone I loved alive and asserting that they had mattered.

I realized that the only way I could truly become a member of the Romemu community would be by joining it, so after the High Holidays I did. I also signed up for an orientation session and for a class in siddur skills taught by Shir Yaakov, Romemu's thirty-something music director. I was hoping to make a friend or two in the class. I thought that if I did, I'd be more likely to consider Romemu my spiritual home.

The problem, of course, was that I continued to lead two separate lives—my life with my family and my life at Romemu. The two seemed quite separate and did not add up to a happy or even satisfying whole. But there were definitely signs of progress. Before the High Holidays, Elizabeth took a one-day class in challah-baking at the Jewish Community Center near her yoga class. That night, we ate the loaf she had baked there at our Friday night family dinner. It was a big hit.

Since then, Elizabeth has been working at home on Fridays so that she can make challah, structuring the entire day around the baking process. She prepares the dough before leaving the house for her 9:00 A.M. yoga class. When she returns ninety minutes later, it's time to knead the dough and roll it into rope-shaped strands for braiding. In the half hour it takes for her to shower and return work calls, the dough completes its second rise. She glazes the loaf with an egg wash and bakes it for twenty minutes, while she checks her email. Then she gives the loaf another glaze and turns it in the oven for another twenty minutes of baking—and more phone calls.

When I asked her why she committed herself to the long, hard work of challah-baking, she said, "It makes me feel as though I'm creating a sanctuary for my family."

I asked her to explain.

"I want our children to feel safe in the world—and connected. I want them to feel that our home is a place of meaning and ritual. And to have a sense of continuity and tradition." She also said that she was conscious, as a mother, of "writing the story" of her children's childhood. "This is one of the memories I want them to carry with them throughout their entire lives."

Elizabeth didn't take up baking challah for my sake. She did it because she wanted to create a nourishing and meaningful legacy for our children. But the ritual has become a small bridge between my two separate lives. I may go alone to Romemu for Friday night services. But I come home to the smell of roast chicken and freshly baked challah, and a meal that begins with the traditional Sabbath blessings over the candles, bread, and wine. It's a start.

part five

Season of Wisdom and Compassion

Love and compassion are necessities, not luxuries.
Without them humanity can't survive.

—THE DALAI LAMA

An Epitaph to Live By

Death is everywhere we turn, throughout all the seasons of our lives. And yet, as I begin this latest season, I am even more aware of it, perhaps as a consequence of getting older and the recent rash of deaths that began with my Aunt Fern and Uncle Pudge.

Three journalist friends died within months of each other. The one I knew best, deeply depressed by a career setback, killed himself three weeks before his fiftieth birthday. Another died at age sixty-two of lung cancer. The third was killed in a car crash; he was only thirty-three.

Shyamdas died, too. He was killed in a motorcycle crash on a winding, hilly road in Goa, India, just before his sixtieth birthday. "How can we live in this world without you?" Jai Uttal wrote on his website. "Are you hiding behind the trees, playing with that cowherd boy [Krishna]? Are you preparing flowers or sweets for His beloved Radharani? Why has He taken you?"

A childhood friend who had always seemed larger than life to me, who was a high school football star and shot-putter, who became a teacher and coach and helped hundreds of kids turn around their troubled lives, died of pancreatic cancer at age sixty-one.

The father of one of Caroline's good friends died of colon cancer at age fifty-two. When Elizabeth told me the news over the phone, I could hear my daughter crying in the background—for her friend but also for herself and every other teenage girl who might lose her father someday.

I just learned about a terrible car crash that killed two sixteen-year-old boys. One of them played on the baseball team I coached a few years ago. The boy who was driving the car worked at a restaurant I go to; he's in a coma.

That's not to count the many friends, relatives, and colleagues who've died in the last year after living into old age, and the ones who are seriously ill. And my octogenarian parents, whose mortality is on my mind each and every day. And the intimations I have several times each day of my own inevitable death.

All this begs the questions: How are we to respond? How are we to live in the face of death?

Some people find solace in the thought that they will be reunited with their loved ones in heaven. (I respect that belief but do not share it.) Others are comforted by the idea that we have a soul that lives on after we die.

I am inspired by what the Reverend F. Washington Jarvis—my high school philosophy teacher—taught: "If you seek to discover the meaning of your life, you have to begin with the one and only thing you can say for certain about your life: You will die."

Jarvis challenged his students to write their own epitaph: "After you die, what would you like people to say about you? Your answer to that question should guide the way you live."

I can't remember the epitaph I wrote for myself in high school, but a few years ago, as I was finishing my first book, I wrote: "In the end, he worked hardest at love."

If you asked me to write one today, as I seek a spiritual identity and home, I'd inscribe this epitaph on my gravestone: "By parenting well, he broke the cycle." By which I mean the cycle of dysfunction that has caused generations of my family so much pain and heartbreak. In its place, I want to create a legacy for my children rooted in the healing power of self-knowledge, empathy, and love.

Here is an example of why I want to break the cycle. It involves the well-meaning people who raised me.

I brought my parents to New York so that they could celebrate their eightieth birthdays with their grandchildren. One afternoon, while I was driving my father to the pharmacy, he told me about his new plan.

"I didn't want to tell you this when your mother might hear. I just made out two checks. Each for $895. That way, you and your brothers won't need to worry about anything."

He was talking about the cost of getting himself and my mother cremated. Since my father is deaf and I was driving, I didn't say anything. I just nodded and kept my eyes on the road.

"Your mother will go first—and it will be quick," he said with certainty. "I looked into buying her a plot next to her mother's grave in Cleveland, but it would have cost you kids five thousand dollars to fly her body there. In Florida, there's a rule that you have to be cremated within two days. With you kids living all over the country, there's absolutely no reason for you to rush there for a funeral."

He had worked it all out.

"When your mother dies, I'll mix her ashes with those of Shana," he said. Shana, my parents' dog, had died ten years earlier; my father kept her ashes on the bookcase in his study. "I've left instructions to add my ashes to Shana's and your mother's when I die, then to put them in four containers, one for each of you boys. Each of you can dispose of our ashes as you wish."

When we got to the pharmacy, I bought a pen and pad of paper and wrote, "Do any of my brothers know about your plan?"

"Not yet," he said. "Ron, Randy, and Roger will be okay with this. But you can get emotional about these things, so that's why I'm telling you first."

"And how about Mom?" I wrote. "Does Mom know that you want to mix her ashes with the dog's ashes and then yours?"

"She'll be fine with it," he said, perturbed with me for asking.

When we got home, I took Elizabeth aside and told her about the conversation I'd just had with my father.

"Are you kidding?" she said. "Your mother will be furious."

Or maybe she'd be fine. However, I didn't want to take a chance; and so, when he went to sleep, I summoned my mother to the kitchen.

"Did you know that Dad is going to mix your ashes with Shana's when you die? He presumes you'll die first. He's left instructions to add his ashes later."

My mother was even angrier than Elizabeth had predicted.

"How dare he?" she fumed. "I didn't even like that dog."

My father's plan was totally in keeping with his values and personality: He loves animals; he likes to keep costs low; if he can keep his checkbook balanced until he dies, he'll be able to rest in peace forever. What horrified my mother and everyone else in the family was that he hadn't factored her wishes into his equation, which is typical, too, for him. I guess that my father's chosen epitaph would be: "I did it my way." As in the song Sinatra made famous: "I faced it all and I stood tall and did it my way." The sentiments of a man who doesn't think he needs anybody else, who belongs to Generation My Way or the Highway.

Don't get me wrong: I love my father. But I hope that my children learn an entirely different lesson from me and Elizabeth: that we need each other from the cradle until the grave in almost everything we do. We especially need each other to learn and grow. To comfort us when we're afraid. To help us nurture our dreams and also our children.

We humans are a species of caretakers, and that's a good thing. We respond to infants crying and to friends, strangers, and animals in need. We are driven to perpetuate ourselves, by which I mean our own DNA and also the whole human race. I hope my children get the pleasure that comes from working with other people toward a common goal and a better future. This will never happen if everyone goes off and just does it their way.

Empathy's Children

I want my children to become empathic listeners and human beings; however, from my own experience, I know that's easier said than done. Considering the hundreds of hours I've spent meditating and praying and trying to internalize Buddha's Four Noble Truths, I still have a precariously short fuse when it comes to certain people and situations. That's why I was lucky to reconnect with my friend Jocelyn Stoller. Without her, I may never have gotten this far in my journey.

I first met Jocelyn in 1979, when I was working as a bartender in Cleveland. Jocelyn was only twenty at the time, but she had already earned her master's degree in educational psychology and traveled around the world to pursue her scholarly interest in belief formation and the human search for meaning. Jocelyn sensed that I was a kindred spirit, so she befriended me.

Night after night, as I poured drinks for my customers, she would hang out at the bar just to have conversations with me. We would discuss our various travels, and she would tell me about her research and experiences of different cultures. I told her about my own spiritual aspirations, which I had abandoned in college after seriously considering converting to Christianity. She intuited that my aspirations were dormant, not dead, and that I'd rekindle them when I was older.

During the 1980s, Jocelyn helped spearhead citizen diplomacy and publishing projects between the United States and the Soviet Union. By 1993, the last time I had seen her, she was co-owner of an early Internet start-up that operated the first major email network with Russia.

Occasionally I'd wonder about Jocelyn—where she was, and what she was doing—but I never made an effort to find her. Then, in 2011, as I started to act on my yearnings for God, a message popped up on my Facebook page: It was Jocelyn asking to "friend" me.

She couldn't have resurfaced at a more auspicious time. Jocelyn, a learning expert, worked on projects that applied the emerging science of brain development to social policies for children and families. She had also continued her study of belief formation, and built a huge interdisciplinary database of books, articles, and research studies in the fields of psychology, anthropology, neuroscience, and systems theory. Altruism, empathy, cults, consciousness, near-death experiences, morality, the evolution of religious myths and rites of passage—these were just a handful of the topics in Jocelyn's treasure trove. When we reconnected, she was busy synthesizing some of this material for book projects and websites on issues that turned out to be directly related to my own search.

When I told her what I was doing, Jocelyn offered to be a support system for me—and to provide an "intellectual context" for whatever I was experiencing. She warned me about the "mental assumptions and cognitive biases" I might be bringing to my spiritual search: how they could cloud my perceptions and hold me back.

Jocelyn had been trained in a variety of mindfulness and self-awareness techniques; she used them to help people process their emotions and move ahead in their lives. "If you're game," she said, "I can use some of these same techniques with you."

I told her my greatest fear: that Elizabeth and I wouldn't be able to bridge our differences about God, and that we'd end up leading two separate lives. "That wouldn't make me happy," I said. "So, yes. I'm game."

During the next two years, as I moved from season to season, Jocelyn and I kept in touch by email and tried to talk every week by phone. Whenever I began a new spiritual practice—for example, meditation, chanting, or davening—she'd send me the latest research on the practice, which helped me understand whether the time I put into it would yield any cognitive, emotional, or health benefits.

Several of Jocelyn's clients had grown up in rigidly fundamentalist households, so she was particularly aware of the damage caused by charismatic leaders and authoritarian religious groups. What concerned Jocelyn in my case was that I might become too cerebral in my search, not seeing the wealth of spiritual knowledge that could be gleaned from my everyday life, or by processing the emotions that came up when something traumatic happened—for example, the death of a friend or an argument with my father. She really helped me recognize the value of that.

We only saw each other once during that time—in San Francisco, when Elizabeth and I were visiting a dear friend who was getting chemotherapy treatments for breast cancer. That weekend, Elizabeth and I went to Yosemite National Park with our friend and her husband. When we got back, I invited Jocelyn to come over to my friend's house to continue exploring some of the techniques we'd been using over the phone. She brought along a protégé—an earnest young man named Gabe, whose role was to massage my head and feet and help Jocelyn put me into a relaxed, receptive state where I could more readily listen and attune to my unconscious.

Before we began the session, we agreed that we would address one of my most vexing core concerns: my views and feelings about God.

Jocelyn explained that, from time to time, Gabe would be tapping gently on my sternum and collarbone—specifically over my vagus nerve. The vagus is one of twelve pairs of cranial nerves that originate in the brain. It passes through the neck en route to the chest and abdomen, connecting to various motor and sensory systems in the diaphragm, stomach, esophagus, and heart. As a result, some researchers have begun using the vagus as a mind-body feedback loop in the treatment of trauma and depression.

There are vagus nerve pacemakers that help with intractable depression, epilepsy, and other conditions. But Jocelyn had been trying techniques that stimulate the vagus directly. By having Gabe tap on my sternum—and occasionally press on the vagus nerve matrix in that area—she hoped to stir up any unconscious feelings I might have about the concept of God.

She instructed me to lie on the floor and on my back, with my eyes closed. Then she counted down slowly from ten to zero. When she reached zero, she said, "Now imagine climbing into the zero and being in a space where you can rest and regenerate and be whoever you are." Then she asked me to visualize the word "God" and tune in to anything else I might be feeling.

Usually I can't visualize anything on command. But now, in this state of almost hypnotic encouragement, the word "GOD" appeared on the inside screen of my eyelids for several seconds. Then the letters *G* and *D* spun off in opposite directions, leaving the letter *O* standing there on its own. The *O* was very similar to the zero Jocelyn had described during her countdown: I crawled into it and felt lighter, freer, and more relaxed. But then I seemed to fall into a tunnel, like Alice careening down the rabbit hole to Wonderland. "I'm spinning out of control," I told Jocelyn. "Now I'm disappearing and I can't feel my body anymore."

"Have you ever experienced this sensation before?" Jocelyn asked.

"Yes," I said. I told her about my LSD trip in high school, how I had hallucinated that I was floating higher and higher into the sky. I had suddenly realized that I was looking down on a coffin that contained my body. It was terrifying. But also exhilarating, like being on a slow-motion rocket ship to a distant star.

Then, as now, I was aware of wanting to escape the limited world of my ego, so that I could become connected to something greater and more enduring.

After I told Jocelyn about my LSD trip, I reflected on what had just happened: The word "GOD" had deconstructed the moment I became aware of the emotions I associated with it.

"In a sense, God doesn't matter," I told her. "I don't mean everything I yearn for in God, just the word."

That one word had been an insurmountable wall between Elizabeth and me. Whenever I said it, Elizabeth would cringe or turn away, eliminating any hope I had that we could coexist spiritually. And yet, we had never really gotten around to exploring what God (by any other name, or no name at all) meant to either of us. We kept getting stuck on semantics.

Jocelyn asked Gabe to keep tapping on my chest, along the vagus nerve. Then she asked me if I had experienced anything else when I crawled through the *O*.

"A desire to heal all the pain in my life." As I said this, I realized that I was talking, in part, about the chronic aches and pains that had been the legacy of my athletic career. These head-to-toe aches distracted me during the day and kept me from sleeping through the night. At the same time, they were shrines to my emotional pain: the pressure I'd felt from parents and coaches; my broken dreams; my fears of reaching out to other people and expressing gratitude or love; my anxieties about failing and also dying. All of these emotions seemed to reside in my swollen joints and tired muscles; in the many places I'd sprained, broken, and torn when I was playing competitive sports.

As I crawled through the tunnel, I imagined being showered with warm, soothing springwater. At the end, when I was drying off and sparkling in the sun, I noticed that there was no more wheezing or heaviness in my chest. No more tingling in my fingers, or numbness in my toes.

I told all of this to Jocelyn; she asked Gabe to begin tapping along my collarbone again.

"Does it bother you that Elizabeth is so certain that there isn't a God?" she asked me.

"Yes and no," I said. "I wish that Elizabeth didn't have such a knee-jerk reaction when I talk about God. But I think she's a lot more open to what I mean by God than she'd like to admit."

I told her about the trip we had taken to Yosemite the day before. When Elizabeth and I were looking up at Half Dome, the granite rock formation that rises nearly five thousand feet above the valley, we talked about how tiny and insignificant it made us feel. Then Elizabeth reached over and held my hand so tenderly that I knew we were experiencing the same ineffable feelings of gratitude and awe.

"Do you think that Elizabeth is worried that you'll take on a belief system that goes counter to her values?" Jocelyn asked.

"I don't think so," I said. "I'm not a fanatical or dogmatic guy. But she does get worried about my obsession with movies like *The Robe* and *Demetrius and the Gladiators*. You can add *Barabbas, Ben-Hur*, and *The Song of Bernadette* to that list. *Zorba the Greek*, too. I'm drawn to stories about courage, where the hero overcomes adversity and persecution and fights for his or her beliefs, especially when there's a soaring and memorable theme song."

I started humming the theme song to *The Robe*; both Jocelyn and Gabe joined in. The film stars Richard Burton as the Roman military tribune who commanded the unit that crucified Jesus. I remembered the first time I saw it—on TV, in 1967, a year after my bar mitzvah. Our family business had just been sold and my relatives were at each other's throats. The movie was full of characters who risked their lives to change the world and do the right thing, which made an impression on my thirteen-year-old self. "Elizabeth might call *The Robe* 'corny,'" I told Jocelyn. "But it was quite inspirational and cathartic for me—and still is."

Jocelyn laughed. "So you want to get to a purer place. Like that Roman tribune who stood at the foot of the cross and became a new man, a saint, the second he clutched the bloodstained robe of Jesus, the man he'd just crucified, to his chest?"

"Exactly." I smiled.

"That's a classic spiritual longing," she said.

I was beginning to see the range of deeply human needs and desires that I had brought to my pilgrimage. I wanted to hurt less. And be loved. I wanted to belong to a community. And be connected to a purpose larger and more enduring than my here-today, gone-tomorrow self. I wanted to be a crusader for everything right and good in the world, and to be a hero to my children.

"Human beings need to create a sense of purpose for their lives.

That's how our brains work. We're meaning generators," Jocelyn said. "Otherwise, we wouldn't be able to handle the gigantic influx of data we're processing—the four hundred billion bits of data per second we get through our senses. And each of us—you, me, Elizabeth, absolutely everyone you know—has a different aesthetic when it comes to their search for meaning. For example, the neural networks that govern your particular search seem to fire up when you hear an inspirational music score or imagine yourself as the protagonist in a great historical epic. How would you describe Elizabeth's aesthetic as compared with your own?"

"Well, she doesn't like to be in situations that require her to be fake," I said. "She gets really impatient with that. She likes all sorts of music, but it needs to be performed well, by people who really know what they're doing. Also, Elizabeth responds best to public speakers who are smart and well informed and teach her something she didn't know before. That's why she liked Sherwin, the rabbi who married us. His sermons always taught her something new about Jewish culture, cuisine, or history. I have a different aesthetic. The sermons I like best tend to be more personal, poetic, and from the heart. They help me think differently about myself and my life, and they inspire me to be more compassionate and giving."

Several other "aesthetic" differences came to mind.

While I like to sit quietly for long periods of time, either thinking or meditating, Elizabeth gets antsy—unless she's got one of our cats on her lap, in which case she's in kitty-mommy heaven. She has a daily yoga practice. She dedicates each session to a friend in need, and she uses yoga to center herself, particularly in times of stress.

Elizabeth has an unbelievably accurate people radar; in a crowded room, she can detect the liars, poseurs, and fools—the genuinely interesting people, too. It's fun to go places with her, because she elevates people-watching (we call it "cultural anthropology") to an art form. While I give almost everyone (except Nazis and serial murderers) the benefit of the doubt, Elizabeth can be brutal, especially when it comes to bigots, braggarts, and Republicans.

"People bring their aesthetic preferences to everything—to religion, too," Jocelyn said. "Romemu might not be Elizabeth's cup of tea. It might be too mystical for her, and put too much emphasis on God. But it's clear that the two of you share a common aesthetic when it comes to the activity that provides by far the most meaning in your lives: parenting. For both of you, parenting is a profoundly spiritual experience, filled with devotion, self-reflection, and joy."

Jocelyn got that right. As parents, Elizabeth and I couldn't be more in sync. Parenting is the great adventure of our lives, and we both know that it would be far less exciting if we were traveling this particular road alone.

We do not parent by teasing, shaming, or punishing our children, or by imperial command. We do it mainly by giving them opportunities to learn and grow. And so our children have a menagerie of pets, play team sports, take violin and piano lessons, enjoy and look forward to all sorts of family gatherings and rituals during the year. They know that we will come to all their concerts and sporting events and be there to help them with their homework and when they need us to help them navigate their lives.

There is no script for the way we parent—it's instinctive, from the gut, trial and error. We're constantly giving each other feedback so that we can do it better.

By working hard at it, we've become much more attuned to what our children need beyond the constant drumbeat they hear (from us and society at large) to achieve and get into college: They also need to move their bodies, chill with friends, encounter nature, reflect on their lives. They need a lot of sleep, which means a lot less screen time. That's our biggest challenge: to persuade them that they've got to give their cell phones and computers a break.

Nothing makes us happier than to see our kids reaching out to comfort or help another person—not because they feel obliged to, or for the brownie points, but because they know, in their heart, that it's the right thing to do. When their Grandma Joyce was in the nursing home with Alzheimer's disease—and didn't know their names—they visited her almost every day. Noah proposed bringing our dogs Pip and Mac along, knowing how much pleasure they'd give to the patients there—and they did.

For years, Caroline has been emailing my father every morning before she goes to school; her daily updates remind him that, even though he's deaf and feeling cut off from the world, she cares. Ben works with autistic children. It challenges and exhausts him. But in a funny way, he says, it lessens the distance he feels from all people who are different from him—and he's grateful for that.

The empathy I see in my children lifts my spirit and softens my heart. Elizabeth and I try to consciously model that kind of behavior for them. They see us being the emotional first responders for any friend or neighbor who suffers an illness or loss. They see us offering to take our friends to their doctors' appointments and babysit their pets and children, whatever they need us to do. If our kids have questions—as Caroline did when her friend's father was dying of colon cancer—we answer as honestly and accurately as we can. At the same time, we try to help our children understand and express how tragic situations like that are making them feel.

I remember my own childhood as being filled with secrets, mysteries, and revenge. My parents taught me to keep up my guard and be wary of other people. My relatives held grudges to the grave. Empathy requires listening deeply to other people, and not letting your inherited craziness get in the way. It entails removing your mask and being vulnerable. It means being able to feel another person's pain, so that you can really walk in that person's shoes and help them. My children are learning to do that, breaking the cycle that caused me and their ancestors so much pain.

The fact is, we humans are wired to empathize. As neuroscientist V. S. Ramachandran of the University of California, San Diego, points out, the mirror neurons in our brain mean that we have a similar response to other people's pain as we do when we respond to our own. Social psychologist Dachner Keltner of the University of California, Berkeley, has conducted studies that show that when people perform behaviors associated with compassionate love—for example, smiling and gesturing in a way that conveys friendliness and warmth—their bodies produce more oxytocin, sometimes called the "bonding" hormone.

I asked Jocelyn what this means in terms of parenting. She said, "From the very beginning of life, neurohormones such as oxytocin, vasopressin, and prolactin weave bonds between parent and child—forming the physiological basis for feelings of connection, familiarity, trust, and belonging. When a child sees his parents acting with compassion and showing respect to other people, that behavior is imprinted in the child.

"As the brain matures," she went on, "a young person acquires the capacity to regulate and cope with a variety of emotional states. He develops the ability to direct his behavior thoughtfully and with concern for how it will impact other people." The circle of empathy gets wider and wider, she said. "Emotionally healthy people have empathic imagination. They can recognize the humanity of people who don't belong to their tribe, religious institution, or family."

You don't have to be a kid to develop empathy; you can do it at any age, thanks to the plasticity of the brain. As we respond to new experiences, changes occur in terms of the number, function, and interconnections of cells in the brain, according to psychology professor Richard J. Davidson of the University of Wisconsin–Madison. Davidson is using meditation and various other techniques to enhance pro-social behavior such as empathy, altruism, and kindness. Just imagine: If more of us learn to become empathic—and if we model empathic behavior for our children—we might end up with a healthier, more peaceful planet, where human behavior is dictated less and less by the emotionally "primitive" parts of our brain.

Epilogue: The Days of Awe

When I set off on my journey to find a spiritual home, I was fifty-seven years old. I identified strongly with the Jewish people but didn't feel a spiritual connection to my birthright religion. I had some religious inclinations and beliefs, but few of them were set in stone, outside of the discomfort I felt around people who professed One Path or One Truth or the superiority of their way to the exclusion or detriment of others.

At the beginning, I identified several religions that seemed aligned with my values and beliefs, and explored two of them in some depth—liberal Quakerism and Mahayana Buddhism. I was drawn toward their contemplative practices and the way they helped their adherents lead a more ethical life. Later, I found myself worshipping among Hindus and Hasidic Jews, groups that had been near the bottom of my initial list. I was intrigued by their devotional practices and by the way their rituals were designed to praise God and mark the rhythms of the week and seasons.

During my nearly two years of shopping for God, I have grown to understand how deeply human beings yearn to belong, connect, experience transcendence, leave a legacy, and find a purpose for their lives. I do not think that you need a God, a religion, or a spiritual practice to do that. You can achieve an ethical, meaningful, and empathic life as an atheist or agnostic. Many people I know bring a spiritual level of engagement to the work they do, or to their excursions in nature, or to their dedication to a cause. The search for meaning follows a billion paths.

The paths I followed led to a movement that wove Torah study, meditation, ecstatic chanting, and devotional prayer into a context that made the religion to which I was born more compelling to me. I am spending the Jewish High Holidays this year in the company of other Jews who share that aesthetic.

Actually, I no longer think of Rosh Hashanah and Yom Kippur as High Holidays or even as High Holy Days. I think of them as being part of the "Days of Awe" ("Yamim Noraim" in Hebrew). That phrase reflects the high-stakes nature of the soul-searching Jews are supposed to do for ten days, starting with Rosh Hashanah and ending with Yom Kippur. It also conveys the anxiety we're supposed to feel in that time. According to Jewish tradition, Rosh Hashanah is when God determines "who shall live and who shall die" during the coming year. The righteous get inscribed in the Book of Life, the wicked in the Book of Death. But since most of us are neither fully righteous nor fully wicked, we have until Yom Kippur to repent. Then our fate is sealed.

The stakes can't get much higher than that.

Before Yom Kippur, Jews are supposed to seek forgiveness from those they've wronged. For my book *Unfinished Business*, I spent a whole year making amends and repairing the broken relationships in my life. In a sense, it was an extended Yom Kippur—a year of atonement. But I now understand how we need that level of soul-searching every year, whether we're religious or not. The Days of Awe are meant to keep Jews humble. They help us renew our spirit and heal our relationships. They spur us to compassionate action, so that we can begin again, become whole again, and deepen our commitment to serving humanity and God.

On Yom Kippur, Jews are forbidden to eat, drink, bathe, anoint themselves, engage in sexual relations, or wear leather shoes. The hardest part is the fasting; hence, before the holiday begins we wish each other an "easy fast." Fasting helps us focus our attention inward; just as important, it attunes us to the millions of people who go to sleep hungry each night, and our moral obligation to help feed them.

When I was a teenager, I always fasted and attended services on Yom Kippur—out of respect for my grandparents, but also because there was something undeniably sacred about the day. I give my own children a choice, hoping (when they choose not to go to services with me) that they'll at least limit their activities. They never do. Does that sadden me? A little. But it is what it is, as Elizabeth likes to say, and I try to make the best of it after letting my preferences be known.

A week before the most recent Days of Awe began, I gave Noah a list of former and current major-league baseball players who have chosen not to play on Yom Kippur. I gave him the same list last year. It includes Hall of Famers Hank Greenberg and Sandy Koufax (who famously refused to pitch the first game of the 1965 World Series because it fell on Yom Kippur), and also Ken Holtzman, Kevin Youkilis, and Shawn Green.

Noah decided that there was no way his baseball team could win without him. So, like his brother before him, he decided to spend Yom Kippur on the ball field, with Elizabeth and Caroline watching him from the stands. Ben chose to stay home, so that he could hang out with his friends.

Why didn't I insist that the kids go to services with me? Because I knew that forcing them to do so would poison them against doing it later in their lives, when it might have real meaning for them. I really believe that.

On Friday afternoon, before I left for the Presbyterian church that hosts Romemu's services, I grabbed some leftover kale salad from the refrigerator and ate my last meal before the fast. Then I looked through my closet for something white to wear, as is traditional on Yom Kippur eve. I found a white linen shirt and the white cotton suit I wore to the twins' b'nai mitzvah. (White symbolizes purity. Some Jews wear a kittel, in which the Jewish dead are traditionally buried.) Luckily, the pants fit without a belt—so I didn't need to violate the prohibition against leather. I put on a white yarmulke, a pair of white athletic socks, and a pair of faded gray sneakers. Then I walked to shul.

I got there just in time for the chanting of the Kol Nidre, the opening prayer of Yom Kippur. Kol Nidre is actually a legal formula, written in Aramaic: It proclaims null and void the vows and promises that we may make and fail to fulfill in the coming year. The song gets its emotive power from its long opening note, which falls to a lower note before rising again, and conveys an unbearably primal, mournful sigh. Whenever I hear that haunting melody, my eyes well up, as I remember Aunt Fern and my grandparents. So do the eyes of everyone else at the service, as they recall and mourn their own loved ones.

Kol Nidre is followed by five services: one at night and four during the day. At each service, the congregation rises for the viddui, or confessional, where it is customary to beat your chest gently as you recite each sin. This year, I was conscious of beating my chest along the vagus nerve, with the intention of turning my penitential words into heartfelt acts of compassion.

Rabbi Ingber prefaced his Yom Kippur sermon with a poem by Rumi, the thirteenth century Persian poet, theologian, and Sufi mystic. In a mellifluous voice that softened into a whisper, he said:

Come, come, whoever you are.
Wanderer, worshipper, lover of leaving,
It doesn't matter.
Ours is not a caravan of despair.
Come, even if you have broken your vows a thousand times.
Come, yet again, come, come.

After he recited the poem, Ingber told us a story he'd heard about an elderly Jewish woman named Goldie who lived in Brooklyn. One afternoon, Goldie walked into a travel agency and said that she wanted to go to India. The travel agent tried to discourage her: "Why India?" she asked. "It's filthy there, you'll hate the food, you'll get sick and end up in a hospital, there won't be any Jewish doctors there." She offered to find Goldie a reasonable fare to a more enjoyable destination. But Goldie insisted on India.

When she finally got there, after a very long plane ride, Goldie set off for an ashram in the jungle. It took her several grueling days by train and rickshaw to get there. When she did, Goldie told the young devotee at the gate that she wanted to see the guru right away. "But there are hundreds of people waiting in line to see him, to get his blessing," the young man said. "Really, wouldn't you rather go back to Mumbai and go shopping, see the sights, and stay in a nice hotel?"

"No," Goldie said. "I'm here to see the guru."

Goldie waited in line for two days to see the holy man. Another devotee told her that she'd only have time to say three words to the guru, so she should pick her words carefully.

"I'll pick them carefully," Goldie promised.

At long last, it was Goldie's turn to enter the guru's inner sanctum. The guard at the door reminded her, "Only three words."

"No problem," Goldie said. "Just three words."

Now Goldie was standing before the long-haired guru, who looked resplendent in his floor-length saffron robe. Most of the people who passed through this portal prostrated themselves at the guru's feet, then got his blessing. But Goldie would have none of that. She walked to within a foot of the guru. Then she crossed her arms and fixed her gaze. "Sheldon," she said in the commanding voice of everyone's Jewish mother. "Come home."

After all those hours of fasting and penitence, the thousand or so people who were listening to the story exploded with laughter. When the tumult died down, Ingber looked around the room and revealed the point of the story and his sermon: "We're all Sheldon," he said. "We are wanderers, worshippers, and lovers of leaving, who are called home."

As he said this, my entire pilgrimage passed before my eyes, including all the Sheldons of various religious backgrounds I'd encountered at the Morningside and Bulls Head–Oswego Meetings and at Tibet House, Omega, and the Isabella Freedman Jewish Retreat Center; Sharon Salzberg and Bodhisattva Joe; Shyamdas, Krishna Das, and the kirtan wallahs; Reb Zalman and Rabbi Ingber: All of them were lovers of leaving, who had been called home.

In his sermon, Ingber mentioned a distinction that Princeton sociologist Robert Wuthnow had made about America's changing religious landscape since World War II. According to Wuthnow, the 1950s produced a "dweller-oriented" spirituality that mirrored the values and structure of the suburban family. Most Americans stayed within the comfortable confines of their birthright religions, and viewed their churches and synagogues as "safe havens amid the growing uncertainties in the world" brought on by the Cold War and the nuclear arms race. This was how I was brought up in suburban Cleveland, at the large Conservative synagogue where the rabbi thundered on about the importance of supporting Israel and marrying within the faith so that the Jewish people could survive the threats of intermarriage, assimilation, and another Holocaust.

During the 1960s, an era of political and social unrest that pitted parents against children all across America but particularly on the two coasts, young people appropriated practices, symbols, and beliefs from Eastern religions, New Age therapies, the modern recovery movement, and whatever else served their need for healing, self-discovery, and community. That's what I did in the late 1960s and early 1970s, when my family (for financial reasons) was falling apart, and the Vietnam War led me to question the black-and-white, us-versus-them worldview of my upbringing. I looked beyond my birthright religion for spiritual nourishment.

Wuthnow called it "seeker-oriented" spirituality. Or, as Ingber put it in his sermon, "The dwellers gave way to the seekers, the Sheldons." But in the last decade, there has been another trend. As more and more Americans have been declaring themselves unaffiliated, according to Pew's survey of the American religious landscape, innovators like Ingber and his counterparts in other traditions have been creating authentic spiritual experiences that are starting to bring the seekers home.

During Ingber's Yom Kippur sermon, as I listened to him speak so eloquently to the Sheldon in me, I wondered about the spiritual journeys my own children would (or would not) take. Whenever I ask Ben about his religious identity, he says, "I'm a Jew and an atheist. But more than anything else, I'm a New Yorker." Noah and Caroline agree: They view themselves as being New Yorkers first. That's not surprising. When Elizabeth and I met at the bar of the Gramercy Park Hotel on our first date, we described ourselves according to the shaping nature of where we were raised: Detroit meets Cleveland. The God talk came later, way after we got to know each other by discussing our careers, favorite sports teams, and mutual friends.

Although they don't have an extensive Jewish education, my children will have all been educated enough to become b'nai mitzvah. It's clear that they look forward to our Friday night Shabbat dinners, and I wouldn't be surprised if they continue this Jewish and family ritual when they're adults. Will they ever feel compelled to seek out another religion, or develop a more serious relationship with their own? I'm not sure. At the moment, their need to belong and feel connected seems to be satisfied by their friendships and relationships within our extended family. Their need for affiliation is taken care of by school and their membership on sports teams. Their search for meaning is subsumed by homework, extracurricular activities, and the demands of getting into college.

However, all that could change in a heartbeat: if one of the people closest to them, beyond their remaining grandparents, gets seriously ill or dies; or the technology that connects them to their friends and so much else leaves them feeling overwhelmed, isolated, and empty. Life's ups and downs may start them pondering life's meaning. Or they may be humbled as they realize how little they can perceive and know as human beings, opening themselves up to at least the possibility of a God.

Perhaps they'll feel a sudden need to cry out in prayer. Or they'll get a glimpse of something so beautiful, inexplicable, and awe-inspiring that they'll be moved to praise whatever and whomever might have been responsible for creating it. Perhaps that something will be the birth of their own children, part of a chain of births that stretches back in time, having been experienced by billions of human beings, who will continue to experience each new birth as though it's the first, miraculous birth in the history of the world. When my children have children of their own, perhaps they'll feel a primal desire to explore their birthright religion, or perhaps they will not.

My children may end up becoming dwellers or seekers, something else or nothing at all. It really doesn't matter to me. As long as they lead empathic, meaning-filled lives.

I have come home to a community of Jews who worship in a Presbyterian church just five blocks away from where I live. I traveled a long and winding road to get here. But isn't that always the case? Our true spiritual lives take place each and every day—in the streets, at our schools, in our workplaces, and around the dining room table—as we interact with other people. We grow in wisdom not by gazing at our navels, but by responding to the trials and tribulations, the uncertainties and tragedies that define our fragile human condition, helping us to see (as the Quakers say) "that of God in every person." In this sense, everywhere we focus our moral, ethical, and empathic attention is a stop on our pilgrim's journey to become a better human being. And the Season of Wisdom and Compassion goes on and on until we die.

In summing up Yom Kippur, Ingber said, "We dress and re-hearse our deaths, in white shrouds," so that "we can use death as a goad to living well, and to claiming a life lived well as the ultimate value."

It's an idea that resonates with me. I bet it will with Elizabeth, too.

Acknowledgments

To Hudson Street Press, especially Caroline Sutton, for acquiring, publishing, and championing this book, and Christina Rodriguez, for being such an astute and supportive editor.

To my agent David Black, for bringing his considerable passion and skills to this project.

To my friends Sara Brzowsky, Kate Edgar, Donna Jackson, and Janice Levine, for reading the manuscript and suggesting improvements that reflected their different perspectives and areas of expertise.

To Miranda Barry, Walter Beebe, Rabbi Lester Bronstein, Jason Ray Brown, Henry Buck, Arthur Bushkin, Marc Byrnes, Shana Deane, Rayne Edelbrock, Rabbi Fred Elias, Theresa Edwards, Shir Yaakov Feit, Dr. Serena Fox, Andrea Gagliardi, Pastor Richard S. Hipps, Robert S. Johnson, Jamie Kaplan, Mardi Kendall, Michael Lesy, Dan Magida, Dr. Tyler Miller, Monica Nataraj, Andre Parhamovich, Gabriel Parulis, Liz Perle, Rick Porter, Steve Pressman, Anna Rayne-Levi, Tia Riemenschneider, Robert Sachs, Dr. Oliver Sacks, Arthur H. Samuelson, Trip Sinnott, Ernie Sites, Lilian Van

Dam, Ralph White, and Emma Whitmore, for conversations, correspondence, and encounters that pushed and encouraged me.

To the many teachers and visionaries who nurtured and inspired me spiritually over the years, especially through our work together: Reverend F. Washington Jarvis, Reverend William Sloane Coffin Jr., John Hersey, Jaroslav Pelikan, Ansel Adams, Henri Cartier-Bresson, Sister Isolina Ferré, Aung San Suu Kyi, Rabbi Abba Hillel Silver, Rabbi Sherwin Wine, Philip Toshio Sudo, Elie Wiesel, Archbishop Chrysostomos of Etna, and Bishop Auxentios of Photiki.

To the wise men and women at the center of this book: Katherine Alford, Sharon Salzberg, Joe Loizzo, Krishna Das, Shyamdas, Radhanath Swami, Faith Linda Weissman, Claude Stein, Reb Zalman Schachter-Shalomi, Rabbi Arthur Waskow, Rabbi David Ingber, and Jocelyn Stoller. I am grateful to have encountered you at important crossroads of my journey. I hope that my reporting has conveyed the spirit and integrity of your words and ideas.

To the Morningside and Bulls Head–Oswego Meetings, Romemu, Omega Institute, the Cathedral of Saint John the Divine, Riverside Church, Ananda Ashram, Union Theological Seminary, Tibet House, the Isabella Freedman Jewish Retreat Center, the NYU Center for Spiritual Life, and the basilicas of Montserrat and Sagrada Família, for providing sacred spaces that welcome seekers of all faiths to experience what they need, whether it be a sense of community or the silence that helps us hear the voice within.

And finally: to my parents; to my brothers Randy, Ron, and Roger; to Elizabeth and our children Ben, Caroline, and Noah, for working so hard and so courageously to create a new legacy.

Bibliography

There were hundreds of books that provided me with guidance and inspiration as I searched for God and a spiritual home. The following were particularly helpful in the research and writing of this book.

The Bhagavad Gita: Krishna's Counsel in Time of War. Trans. Barbara Stoler Miller. New York: Bantam Classics, 1986.

The Desert Fathers: Sayings of the Early Christian Monks. Trans. Benedicta Ward. London: Penguin Books, 2003.

The Evergetinos: A Complete Text. Trans. Archbishop Chrysostomos and Hieromonk Patapios. Etna, CA: Center for Traditionalist Orthodox Studies, 2008.

Faith and Practice: The Book of Discipline of the New York Yearly Meeting of the Religious Society of Friends. New York: Religious Society of Friends, 2008.

How to Be a Perfect Stranger: The Essential Religious Etiquette Handbook. Woodstock, VT: Skylight Paths Publishing, 2003.

Sacred Writings. Ed. Jaroslav Pelikan. New York: Quality Paperback Book Club, 1992.

Judaism: The Tanakh. New York: Jewish Publication Society, 1988.

Christianity: The Apocrypha and the New Testament. New York: Oxford University Press and Cambridge University Press, 1989.

Buddhism: The Dhammapada. Trans. John Ross Carter and Mahinda Palihawadana. New York: Oxford University Press, 1987.

Hinduism: The Rig Veda. Trans. Ralph T. H. Griffith. New York: Motilal Banarsidass Publishers, 1992.

Islam: The Qur'an. Trans. Ahmed Ali. New York: Princeton University Press, 1988.

The Torah: A Modern Commentary. Ed. W. Gunther Plaut. New York: Union of American Hebrew Congregations, 1981.

The Way of the Pilgrim and the Pilgrim Continues His Way. Trans. Helen Bacovcin. New York and London: Image Books/Doubleday, 1978.

The World Treasury of Modern Religious Thought. Ed. Jaroslav Pelikan. Boston: Little, Brown, 1990.

The Yoga Sutras of Patanjali. Trans. Sri Swami Satchidananda. Yogaville, VA: Integral Yoga Publications, 1978.

Alter, Robert, *The Book of Psalms: A Translation with Commentary.* New York: W. W. Norton, 2007.

Armstrong, Karen, *Buddha.* New York: Viking Penguin, 2001.

Bill, J. Brent, *Holy Silence: The Gift of Quaker Spirituality.* Brewster, MA: Paraclete Press, 2005.

Buber, Martin, *I and Thou.* Trans. Ronald Gregor Smith. New York: Scribner Classics, 2000.

Burton, Robert A., *On Being Certain: Believing You Are Right Even When You're Not.* New York: St. Martin's Press, 2008.

Das, Krishna, *Chants of a Lifetime: Searching for a Heart of Gold.* Carlsbad, CA: Hay House, 2010.

Dass, Baba Ram, *Be Here Now.* San Cristobal, NM: Lama Foundation, 1971.

Epstein, Greg M., *Good Without God: What a Billion Nonreligious People Do Believe.* New York: Harper, 2010.

Falk, Marcia, *The Book of Blessings: New Jewish Prayers for Daily Life, the Sabbath and the New Moon Festival.* New York: Harper-Collins, 1996.

Fox, George, *An Autobiography.* Ed. Rufus M. Jones. Richmond, IN: Friends United Press, 2006.

Freud, Sigmund, *The Future of an Illusion.* Ed. James Strachey. New York: W. W. Norton, 1975.

Heschel, Abraham Joshua, *The Sabbath: Its Meaning for Modern Man.* Boston: Shambala, 2003.

Jung, C. G. *Memories, Dreams, Reflections.* New York: Vintage Books, 1963.

Khan, Hazrat Inayat, *The Music of Life: The Inner Nature and Effects of Sound.* New Lebanon, NY: Omega, 2005.

Lewis, C. S., *Mere Christianity.* New York: HarperCollins, 2001.

Newberg, Andrew, and Mark Robert Waldman, *Why We Believe What We Believe: Uncovering Our Biological Need for Meaning, Spirituality, and Truth.* New York: Free Press, 2006.

Phillips, J. B., *Your God Is Too Small.* New York: Macmillan, 1961.

Prabhupada, A. C. Bhaktivedanta Swami, *Sri Isopanisad: The Knowledge That Brings One Nearer to the Supreme Personality of Godhead, Krishna.* New York: Bhaktivedanta Book Trust, 1974.

Radhakrishnan: Selected Writings on Philosophy, Religion, and Culture. Ed. Robert A. McDermott. New York: E. P. Dutton, 1970.

Robinson, John A. T., *Honest to God*. Philadelphia: Westminster Press, 1963.

Rosen, Steven J., *The Yoga of Kirtan: Conversations on the Sacred Art of Chanting*. Nyack, NY: Folk Books, 2008.

Sacks, Oliver, *Musicophilia: Tales of Music and the Brain*. New York: Vintage Books, 2007.

Sarasvati, Shri Brahmananda, *Nāda Yoga: The Science, Psychology and Philosophy of Anahata Nada Yoga*. Monroe, NY: Baba Bhagavandas Publication Trust, 2007.

Siegel, Daniel J., *Mindsight: The New Science of Personal Transformation*. New York: Bantam Books, 2010.

Smith, Huston, *The Religions of Man*. Scarborough,: Harper & Row, 1965.

Tillich, Paul, *Dynamics of Faith*. New York: Harper & Row, 1957.

Tsering, Geshe Tashi, *The Four Noble Truths: The Foundations of Buddhism*, vol. 1. Somerville, MA: Wisdom Publications, 2005.

Wine, Sherwin T., *Judaism Beyond God: A Radical New Way to Be Jewish*. Farmington Hills, MI: Society for Humanistic Judaism, 1985.

Zaleski, Philip, and Carol Zaleski, *Prayer: A History*. Boston: Houghton Mifflin, 2005.